Happy Birthday
Harry!

Lots of love,
David + Jane

Sequoia

Sequoia cruising off the New Jersey coast. Courtesy Ann Stevens.

Sequoia
Presidential Yacht

Giles M. Kelly
Captain, USNR (Ret.)

With Photographs by Ann Stevens

Tidewater Publishers
Centreville, Maryland

Library of Congress Cataloging-in-Publication Data

Kelly, Giles M.,
Sequoia : presidential yacht / Giles M. Kelly ; with photography by Ann Stevens.— 1st ed.
p. cm.
Includes bibliographical references and index.
ISBN 0-87033-561-8
1. Sequoia (Yacht) 2. Sequoia (Yacht)—Pictorial works. 3. Presidential yachts—United States—History. 4. Presidents—Homes and haunts—United States—History. 5. Presidents—United States—History. 6. Presidents—United States—Biography. I. Title.
E176.1.K415 2004
387.2'314—dc22
2004015205

Printed in China
First edition

To all who have sailed aboard *Sequoia*
and to all who have helped keep her viable

Sequoia outward-bound on the Washington Channel passing Hains Point. Courtesy Ann Stevens.

A private moment between Presidents Nixon and Brezhnev on *Sequoia*'s upper deck. Courtesy Nixon Presidential Materials Staff of the National Archives.

Contents

Foreword: America's Great Ship

As I look out from the Navy Museum at the Washington Navy Yard waterfront, I am reminded of the great presidential yachts that once moored here at Pier One. For just over one hundred years, the navy provided a specific vessel for the use of the president for national business or recreation. It is a pleasure to have the beautiful yacht *Sequoia* occasionally visit the Navy Yard to lend her elegance again to her former home port—the historic home port of all of the nation's presidential yachts.

The first, in 1874, was the fast steamer *Despatch,* whose wreck is still in the surf at Assateague Island, Virginia. *Dolphin,* the fourth ship of the navy's new all steel fleet in the nineteenth century, was the only yacht sold for scrap, just after WWI. The elegant yacht *Sylph* was last seen in New York City as a tour boat at the 1939 World's Fair. The largest presidential yacht of all was the magnificent *Mayflower,* serving presidents for an amazing twenty-four years. She ended her days as a passenger ship in the new state of Israel in 1950.

Three presidential yachts still exist and continue to draw interest. Franklin Roosevelt's sleek white *Potomac* had an extensive restoration and is carrying passengers in Oakland, California. The large yacht *Williamsburg* that served Presidents Truman and Eisenhower—the ship that has held my interest for over twenty years—lies as a hulk in Italy after two failed attempts at resurrection in the United States and Europe. *Sequoia,* the sole preserved presidential yacht and the longest serving in the U.S. Navy, is now privately owned and available for charter.

The hot Washington summers convinced many presidents that the waters of the Potomac River provided relief from the pre–air-conditioned White House. The navy vessels chosen for the presidents' use were primarily noncombatant vessels selected for their human comforts. The use of the term "presidential yacht" for these vessels resulted from Navy Undersecretary Theodore Roosevelt acquiring the newly built yacht *Sylph* in 1898 for gunboat duty in the Spanish-American War. Because the yacht was not completed for duty until after the war was over, Roosevelt suggested it be assigned for the sole use of President McKinley and be kept at the Washington Navy Yard. The phrase presidential yacht has stuck to these vessels ever since. Roosevelt himself commissioned the largest of all presidential yachts, *Mayflower,* for his use in 1902.

The United States Navy Museum holds the most complete archive of the presidential yachts. Yet little remains of these great ships in artifacts or materials used aboard. And no museum exhibit could duplicate the experience of being aboard the president's own vessel. This is the great value of *Sequoia:* allowing today's citizens to walk the decks of their leaders' ship.

The importance of Captain Kelly's book is in telling the story of this national landmark vessel–not only the stories of the ship's place in naval architecture, politics, and the personal lives of our chief executives and business moguls, but also its place in history, its triumphs and challenges, and its return to Washington, D.C. There is no better author to tell this tale than Captain Kelly, a retired naval officer and sailor of our local Anacostia and Potomac Rivers, who took *Sequoia* on her greatest voyage—the circumnavigation in 1984 of the eastern United States. Under Captain Kelly's command, *Sequoia* was kept shipshape and run "navy style."

It is hoped that the commitment to this great ship's preservation shown by her current owner is carried on by all of her stewards in years to come. She shares a place in history like no other ship. Her current owner has made her available for charter "except when in use by the president." I hope she continues to serve her country in her best capacity in the future.

Enjoy this book on America's grand yacht. In the navy tradition, I wish her fair winds and following seas in her long career to come.

—Kim Nielsen, Director
United States Navy Museum
Washington Navy Yard
Washington, D.C.

Preface

The Presidential yacht *Sequoia* may be the best-known and best-loved yacht in America because of her beautiful design, her unique history, and her fine state of preservation. She has seen glory days and dismal days. She has witnessed distressing political problems and has known some dubious characters, but on the whole *Sequoia* has been a happy ship that many of her former guests and crew members remember with great affection.

Sequoia has provided fun, privacy, comfort, and solace for at least eight presidents. Privacy has been one of her most valued features, for privacy is precious to high-ranking officials in the public eye. She also has provided them with an attractive change of scene. Her history gives some insight into the lives and lifestyles of the people who most used *Sequoia*.

She has been both a private and public stage, but we probably will never know all the drama played out on her decks. The spareness of records has led to speculation and inspired many myths. *Sequoia*'s private owners tended to spin tall tales to impress the public with the importance of their property or to make the yacht seem more noble than she really is.

One such myth is that Franklin Delano Roosevelt and Sir Winston Churchill met on board *Sequoia*. Another is that the carpet in *Sequoia*'s salon is made of silk and is a gift from Chinese General Chiang Kai-shek. I have tried to do reality checks, perhaps at some cost to the yacht's glamour. But I hope the result is a fairly accurate picture of how this unusual yacht has been employed and enjoyed.

The term "yacht" has been a problem for *Sequoia* because some political figures, Presidents Jimmy Carter and Dwight D. Eisenhower among them, believed that close association with anything called a yacht while in office would tarnish their image because it might seem ostentatious. For that reason even today some congressional and administration leaders are reluctant to support her, let alone use her, though she is indeed a very modest yacht for the government of a superpower. At her inception, her designer referred to her not as a yacht, but as a "houseboat."

One problem in assembling *Sequoia*'s history has been the dearth of her logbooks. In the National Archives, only two of her forty-four years of naval service logbooks are to be found. Thus, I have had to rely largely on anecdotal material gathered from former guests and crew and from press reports and published memoirs. Another problem is the apparent loss of her original drawings. On the other hand, I have been privileged to be closely associated with *Sequoia* over a period of twenty years, including the years when I was her skipper from 1983 to 1988. I thus have been able to provide firsthand information about the yacht during that time.

This book is not the complete story of *Sequoia*. At this writing she is seventy-nine years old, one of the oldest of about fifty Trumpy-designed vessels still operational, and she appears to have a future. In any case, this seems an appropriate time to put together what information is available about her past. Many individuals who have known this special vessel have enthusiastically shared with me their memories of her and join with me in hoping this story will help to ensure her preservation and celebration for many years to come.

—G.M.K.
Washington, D.C.

Acknowledgments

I am much obliged to the many former *Sequoia* crew members, some but not all of whom are mentioned by name herein, for providing me with their recollections and memorabilia of their association with the yacht. Without their contributions there would be no book.

I have been greatly helped by consultations with former *Sequoia* skippers including John H. Besson, Jr., R. Kent Rosemont, R. A. "Chic" Bowling, William H. Meanix, Arthur P. Ismay, Andrew J. Combe, and John L. O'Brien.

I have had the unstinted assistance of staff members of the presidential libraries of Hoover, Roosevelt, Truman, Eisenhower, Kennedy, Johnson, and Ford, which I greatly appreciate. Special thanks go to Claudia Jew of the Mariner's Museum, Newport News, Virginia, and Dr. Robert Browning, historian of the Coast Guard.

In particular, I am especially grateful for the support given to me by these friends and colleagues:

- William Codus, who has had a long personal association with the yacht that goes back to the Ford administration when he was deputy chief of protocol at the Department of State. He provided me with invaluable support, humor, and encouragement for this book.
- Andrew Combe, Captain, USN (Ret.), a former skipper of *Sequoia* who generously supplied me with important technical and historical information.
- James Ernsberger, who organized a timely reunion of *Sequoia* alumni and encouraged them to provide photos and stories for my research and writing of the book.
- Kim Nielsen, director of the Navy Museum in Washington, D.C., who provided me with advice and enthusiasm when it was most needed.
- Gary Silversmith, who generously gave me access to his yacht and his presidential memorabilia.
- Anthony "Tony" Wells, shipmate, skipper, and friend, who taught me much about *Sequoia* and contributed time and thought to this story.

My special thanks also go to the William Killgellen Foundation and the Lloyd and Mabel Johnson Foundation for their interest in having a fully illustrated book produced about *Sequoia,* and to Captain Todd Creekman, USN (Ret.), director of the Naval Historical Foundation, for his key institutional support.

Last, but certainly not least, my most grateful thanks go to my wife Ann Stevens, who urged me in the first place to write this book, then helped me collect information, supplied many of the photographs from her collection, and served as the photo editor for this book. Along the way, she also guided me through editorial intricacies and computer complexities. However, I must plead *mea culpa* for all shortcomings herein.

—G.M.K.

The original 85-foot *Sequoia* at launching in Camden, New Jersey, in 1925.

Members of the Cadwaladers' *Sequoia II* crew.

CHAPTER ONE

A Fashionable Age of Yachting, 1923–29

Teakwood and mahogany were splattered with real champagne yesterday . . . when Mrs. Richard M. Cadwalader christened the new $200,000 yacht Sequoia II.

—*Philadelphia Public Ledger*, October 10, 1925

The decade of the 1920s was a fashionable time for yachting because many wealthy families were showing off their big yachts. The Jazz Age was in full swing and flappers danced the Charleston. Prohibition was in force, F. Scott Fitzgerald was in vogue, and George Gershwin had just composed *Rhapsody in Blue*.

The Cadwaladers and Their Yachts

The story of *Sequoia* begins with a light in a fashionable lady's eye. The year was 1924 and the place Philadelphia. The lady was Emily Roebling Cadwalader, a woman of considerable wealth in her own right, who was married to prominent banker Richard M. Cadwalader, Jr. As a leading member of Philadelphia's high society, Emily Cadwalader often was mentioned in the social pages of both the New York and Philadelphia newspapers. Her grandfather had built the Brooklyn Bridge. Her brother had gone down with the *Titanic*.

The Cadwaladers took delivery of their first Trumpy-designed yacht in 1923, a modest 85-footer they named *Sequoia*. There is no record of why they chose that name. Perhaps because of the Native American Sequoyah who created the Cherokee alphabet or perhaps in recognition of the giant sequoia trees in California. In any case, *Sequoia* was designed to cruise on the Delaware and Chesapeake Bays during the warm months and to sail to Florida for the colder ones by way of the Intracoastal Waterway. But that first *Sequoia* was barely a year old when Emily decided the yacht was not grand enough for the Cadwaladers' station in life. "It was time," the lady said, her eyes shining brightly, "to have a bigger yacht."

In 1924 the Cadwaladers ordered construction of a larger, grander yacht, to be named *Sequoia II.* They had no idea this yacht eventually would become the yacht used by U.S. presidents.

Like her namesake, *Sequoia II* was built just across the Delaware River from Philadelphia in the Mathis Yacht Building Co. at Camden, New Jersey. Her designer was John Trumpy, a renowned naval architect who had emigrated from Norway and had developed a reputation in America for designing luxury, shallow-draft, liveaboard yachts that were marketed as "the Mathis Houseboat Cruisers." Clients included the Du Pont, Guggenheim, Morgan, and Chrysler families. The second Cadwalader yacht was Trumpy hull number 174. She was 104 feet 7 inches long with a beam of 19 feet. Her draft of 4½ feet allowed easy navigation on the Intracoastal Waterway to Florida.

Trumpy's design for *Sequoia II* was particularly distinctive, due to a low overhanging fish deck at her stern and eight portholes forward on each side of the hull. The specifications called for a deckhouse made of Burmese teak finished in varnish. Much of her interior was paneled in Honduras mahogany and walnut. Her design emphasized homelike comforts rather than speed; she had four staterooms, each with an adjoining bath. The wheelhouse was on the main deck. Behind it were a pantry and a combination living room–dining room with curved windows at the forward end. Aft of the deckhouse was a porchlike open deck. At the stern, steps led down to a low fantail deck. Her twin Winton gasoline engines provided a cruising speed of about nine knots and a range of 1,400 miles. Twin 36-inch propellers made her easy to maneuver. *Sequoia II* was delivered in 1925 at a cost of about $200,000.

Trumpy described his design as one that offered a clear expansive deck entirely covered with awnings, where, in comfortable wicker chairs on hot summer days and evenings, guests could enjoy the cooling breeze and have the opportunity to move about with sufficient elbow room. Keeping cool in summer was especially important in those days as air-conditioning was not standard.

Trumpy constructed his yachts with the finest materials available, prompting the *New York Times* to call them "the Rolls-Royces of American yachting." They were considered the top of the line. Trumpy wrote that he hoped his yachts would be able to "make the grand tour of American waters—coastal, canal, lake, and river." Some sixty years later, the yacht he designed for the Cadwaladers, then called just *Sequoia,* did exactly that.

It was during Prohibition when the second Cadwalader yacht was launched, but Emily Cadwalader was pictured in the *Philadelphia Evening Bulletin* breaking a bottle of champagne over the bow of *Sequoia II.* The social pages mentioned the beautiful people who attended the christening and the elegant dinner parties and cruises that followed.

Shortly after her christening, *Sequoia II* sailed down the Intracoastal Waterway to Florida and proudly anchored at Miami Beach with all flags flying. The *Philadelphia Public Ledger* had predicted "the

Sequoia II in 1925 with her boat booms swung forward. ©The Mariners' Museum, Newport News, Virginia.

vessel will be the queen of the Southern waters this season." The Cadwaladers arrived in Palm Beach by way of a private railway car and joined their yacht, but soon, Emily looked around and apparently determined that their brand-new yacht was still not grand enough for them.

No doubt Emily Cadwalader wanted to take a leading role in yachting social circles. Richard Cadwalader was a member of the New York Yacht Club, and his wife was well aware of the size and elegance of the yachts owned by the Kimberlys, Knights, Firestones, and other wealthy families of the time. Even before they had owned *Sequoia II* for a year, Emily Cadwalader ordered a larger yacht, a 185-foot steel vessel she would name *Savarona*. That yacht was soon followed by a still larger one of 265 feet in length. But even that one was not grand enough, and in 1931 the Cadwaladers took delivery of a megayacht.

Built in Germany, the third *Savarona* was 446 feet long and was hailed as the largest private yacht in the world. It seemed the Cadwaladers had finally trumped all the competition. They kept their impressive *Savarona* for seven years, then sold her in 1938 to the Turkish government. She became the Turkish presidential yacht for a brief period, but on November 23, 2000, the *New York Times* reported that *Savarona* was currently in private ownership and was being operated as a charter vessel in Turkey.

Despite the fact that little *Sequoia II* had apparently been considered by the Cadwaladers as too modest for their

Richard and Emily Cadwalader host a luncheon in 1925 aboard *Sequoia II*. Courtesy Arne Hauger.

place in society, the yacht was widely admired for her design and construction, especially for her fine hull lines and her distinctive overhanging fish deck. Although well designed for comfortable cruising on inland waters, she had the disadvantage of not being suitable for ocean passages.

Sequoia II Sold to Dunning

Sequoia II was sold in 1928 to William Dunning, an oil executive from Houston, Texas, who kept her in Galveston Island on the Gulf Coast. On board, he cooled off during the long, hot Texas summers by cruising inside the barrier islands down Mexico way.

In 1998, one of Dunning's nieces, Ellen Crawford, wrote about her childhood experience of cruising aboard *Sequoia II* in the late 1920s: "Every summer we would take the Pullman car from Houston down to Galveston. We filled three drawing rooms. The group consisted of my uncle and aunt, my grandmother, me, and a maid or two. Once we sailed up the coast to New York City where we berthed at the Corinthian Yacht Club as my uncle was a member.

"The ladies shopped and the ship was stocked with food, wines and liquor, and anything else to make the cruise a comfortable one. While this was going on we stayed at the Savoy Plaza [hotel]. Once things were stowed away we started our cruise to Maine and the Canadian border. We fished, went out in the little speed boat, and the ladies paid calls on acquaintances who had summer homes along the way. Truly a life of happy leisure. We spent two or three months on this."

Ellen Crawford also knew that her uncle had taken a trip to Cuba in *Sequoia II* and had visited gambling casinos there. On another occasion he used *Sequoia II* for a business trip to Mexico.

Then came the stock market crash of 1929. Dunning kept *Sequoia II* until March 20, 1931. The Depression had hurt his oil business, and, through a broker, he sold the yacht to the U.S. Department of Commerce for $48,860.

Arne Hauger's Story: An Original Crew Member

On a fine day in March 1984, *Sequoia,* formerly *Sequoia II,* was at the Huckins Yard in Jacksonville, Florida, having work done on her air-conditioning in preparation for summer cruising. An elderly gentleman made his way down the pier to *Sequoia*'s temporary berth. He carried a couple of photo albums under his arm and asked if he could come aboard. He introduced himself as Arne Hauger, eighty-one years old, and one of the original crew members of *Sequoia II* in 1925 when she was launched at Camden, New Jersey. He told this story to crew member and photographer Ann Stevens:

> I was born in Norway near Oslo back in 1902 and went to sea before I was twelve years old. I was a deck boy on a square-rigger and had to do what the other guys didn't want to do. We once rounded Cape Horn and picked up a cargo in China.
>
> After being torpedoed in the First World War, I came to the United States knowing very little English. That was in 1920. For a time I worked digging a 12-foot wide tunnel that was to bring water to New York City from upstate New York, but after a tunnel fire, I quit.
>
> In 1924, I was living with some Italian folks who worked at Mathis shipyard in Camden, New Jersey. That is how I heard about a job there. I went to the yard and was hired as an able-bodied seaman by Captain Brown for a new 85-foot motor yacht called *Sequoia.* The pay was $90 a month. That was twice the normal pay for a seaman. This new yacht was owned by Mr. Richard M. Cadwalader, Jr., of Philadelphia.
>
> But *she* had the money, Miss Emily Roebling did. Her grandfather built the Brooklyn Bridge. When he died, her father finished building it. They were high society. She played the mandolin. I always called her "Madam."
>
> The Cadwaladers were members of the Corinthian Yacht Club. Mr. C. was a Princeton University graduate and about 60 years old when I started working for him.
>
> I'd been with them for two months when we took the yacht to Florida. The Cadwaladers came down to Palm Beach in their private railroad car that they hooked up to a train in Philadelphia. They stayed on board *Sequoia* for three or four weeks and at Christmas gave everyone a $50 bill. They were very generous.
>
> In 1925 the captain said we are going up to look at *Sequoia II.* She is being built for the Cadwaladers at the Mathis yard to Mr. Trumpy's design. When I first saw her, she was inside a shed, just a hull, no deck at all. Later they painted

Crew member Arne Haugeر in 1926 aboard *Sequoia II*. Courtesy Arne Hauger.

her bottom with copper paint and an 8- or 10-inch green boot stripe. The overheads (ceilings) were painted a light green with varnished strips.

Sequoia II made her first test run up to the Columbia Yacht Club on the Hudson River by way of the Delaware and Raritan River Canal. [This 7-foot deep canal carried barge traffic through central New Jersey until 1932, but is no longer in use.] They kept 'little *Sequoia*' a while longer, but all of the original *Sequoia* crew went to *Sequoia II* except for the captain and the chef.

Sequoia II had a crew consisting of a captain, mate, chef, two stewards, two engineers, two sailors, two mess boys, and a maid. The men slept forward. Four slept in the nose, two by the mess table, four across from the captain. The maid slept in the guest area. There was no door then between the galley and the crew's quarters. The new *Sequoia* went south in the fall of 1925 to Miami's Long Key—the easiest fishing place to go to because we could get outside [to the ocean] easily. We caught stone crabs and crawfish—Mrs. C. loved those. I was soon promoted to "fish guide."

The engines of *Sequoia II* were twin gasoline Wintons which were started by compressed air. We had only one generator and one rudder then. [Later the yacht had three rudders.] The chef had a six-burner kerosene stove on the starboard side. One day it caught fire; the flames went sky high, but I was able to put them out with an extinguisher.

On the top deck *Sequoia II* carried two 18-foot launches, one on each side, powered by four-cylinder engines, plus a skiff on the port side. There were three sets of davits. The fall lines could be connected to a winch in back of the stack. The starboard gangway was made out of teak with five brass stanchions and canvas cloth up the sides. We could hoist it in with the davit. All the fittings that are now chrome-plated were brass then. The anchor windlass is not the same. We had smaller anchors and chain. We had toolboxes on both sides of the bow where the gyro repeaters are now. They had leather cushions and were used for seats. We turned off the generator when at anchor because it was noisy, and we used a bank of batteries for power. They were located under a couch that had leather cushions in what is now the after salon.

We covered the wicker furniture every night with canvas slipcovers. We used sponges to varnish the copper window screens so as not to block the holes. The main stateroom then was the after stateroom. We could accommodate seven or eight guests on board. The entrance to the staterooms has been changed. The old entrance was where the bar is now, and a baby grand piano was once where the stairs are now.

Arne Hauger was crew on *Sequoia II* until 1928, when she was put up for sale. Hauger married in 1941. He was drafted into the army in 1942, and while he was in the service, his son was born. Eventually Hauger became a first-class shipfitter, working at the Merrill-Stevens Shipyard in Miami and later at the Naval Air Station in Jacksonville until his retirement. Hauger died in Starke, Florida, in 1991.

USS *Despatch,* circa 1885. Courtesy U.S. Naval Historical Center.

USS *Dolphin,* circa 1893. Courtesy U.S. Naval Historical Center.

CHAPTER TWO

Sequoia's Presidential Predecessors, 1880–1929

I feel that with the demise of the presidential yachts, a great mark of the prestige and luster of the presidency has also vanished, and I am sure many Americans would agree.

—Fred E. Crockett, author, *Special Fleet*

Royal yachts and presidential yachts have been a tradition among maritime nations for centuries. However, the United States has never built a vessel specifically designed as a presidential yacht. Instead the government has converted vessels that were designed for other purposes, such as commerce, war, or private pleasure. The first American presidential yacht was a converted commercial side-wheeler named *River Queen* built in 1864 and chartered for the use of President Abraham Lincoln.

American presidential yachts have served not only for presidential retreats, recreation, and transportation, but also as sites for official entertainment, conferences, ceremonies, receptions, fleet reviews, and, of course, for fishing. These special yachts also were made available for cabinet members, subcabinet officers, and congressional leaders, not just for their pleasure, but also as a place for business.

Presidential Naval Yachts

The first U.S. naval vessel outfitted as an official presidential yacht was a steam-driven warship of 174 feet named USS *Despatch*. After several years overseas operating as a naval quick-dispatch ship, she began her presidential service with President Rutherford B. Hayes, and she later served Presidents Chester A. Arthur and Grover Cleveland. President Arthur was aboard *Despatch* in New York Harbor during the opening of the Brooklyn Bridge on May 24, 1883. *Despatch* also was on hand in Washington for President Cleveland's White House wedding in June 1886 and fired off a twenty-one-gun salute for the occasion. However, in 1891 her presidential service abruptly ended. On her way from New York to Norfolk, she was wrecked on Virginia's Atlantic Coast in an October gale.

USS *Sylph,* circa 1920. Courtesy U.S. Naval Historical Center.

The second naval ship to serve as a presidential yacht was the three-masted steel cruiser USS *Dolphin,* 256 feet in length. She was commissioned in 1885 as part of the "new navy," and she saw duty in both the Atlantic and Pacific Oceans. She was converted in 1892 to the presidential yacht and served as such for Presidents Benjamin Harrison, Grover Cleveland (his second term), William McKinley, and Theodore Roosevelt. Cleveland and his cabinet were on board in 1893 for the Grand Naval Review held in New York Harbor. Being a large ship, she was used more for ceremonial occasions than for presidential recreation. After her long and varied service, *Dolphin* was decommissioned in 1921.

The third naval vessel to serve as a presidential yacht was USS *Sylph,* an attractive smaller ship of 124 feet that was built, armed, and commissioned in 1898. She was assigned to special services at the Washington Navy Yard where President McKinley was the first to use her. However, it was President Theodore Roosevelt who used her most. Between 1901 and 1909 he took frequent cruises, including trips to and from his summer place at Oyster Bay on Long Island Sound. To avoid the Washington heat, President Taft used her off the coast of New England during the summers of his administration. Woodrow Wilson was the last president to use *Sylph.* After she was displaced as the presidential yacht in

USS *Mayflower,* circa 1928. Courtesy U.S. Naval Historical Center.

1921 by USS *Mayflower,* she became the secretary of the navy's yacht and remained in Washington until decommissioned in 1929.

The much larger 318-foot warship *Mayflower* had been built in 1896 as a private yacht, but she was converted to a naval warship in 1898 and saw service in the blockade of Cuba during the Spanish-American War. Later she served as Admiral Dewey's flagship. In 1905, she was converted back into a yacht for President Theodore Roosevelt, who used her extensively during his second administration. *Mayflower* was the site for the signing of the treaty that Roosevelt had mediated to end the Russo-Japanese War. She also served as the presidential yacht for Presidents William Howard Taft, Woodrow Wilson, Warren G. Harding, and Calvin Coolidge. Wilson liked her for ceremonial purposes such as his review of the navy's Great White Fleet. However, Coolidge enjoyed her more for recreation with family and guests.

With the onset of the Depression in 1929, President Herbert Hoover ordered *Mayflower* decommissioned as an economy measure. Her naval career ended at the Philadelphia Navy Yard in 1931, when she suffered serious damage from a fire while being reconverted into a warship. For a time, she returned to private ownership, but when America entered World War II, *Mayflower* was repurchased for use by the Coast Guard as a patrol and training ship. Fire again damaged her, and again she was sold into private hands. After new repairs, *Mayflower* reportedly was used to secretly deliver Jewish refugees to Palestine in 1948, thus capping the career of this once grand and versatile ship.

After *Mayflower* was decommissioned, Hoover was without a designated presidential yacht. He borrowed *Sequoia* from the Department of Commerce in 1931, thus marking the beginning of *Sequoia's* presidential history. When she was commissioned in 1933 for the use of President Franklin Delano Roosevelt, *Sequoia* became the fifth and smallest in the line of official presidential yachts.[1]

CHAPTER THREE

First Call to Presidential Service, 1931–35

It is such a lovely afternoon. I have stayed on board, partly to sleep and partly to get the last mail accumulation off my hands. The Sequoia *is as lovely as ever—even lovelier.*

—Lou Hoover, December 24, 1932

Each president used *Sequoia* in his own special style, and most seemed to see her as offering a cool and convenient change of pace and scenery from the White House. Some favored her as a private retreat, others as a "back room" for political purposes, and some for social purposes such as entertaining colleagues and foreign visitors. Several presidents used her for all of these reasons. For a full picture of life aboard *Sequoia* perspectives from both the "upper deck" and the "lower deck" are needed.

President Herbert Hoover, 1931–32

During the Depression years, public criticism was expressed over the expense of the presidential yacht *Mayflower*. Without a strong need by the president for such a big yacht, the cost of keeping her active was hard to justify. Thus in 1929, as an economy measure to save some $300,000 a year, President Hoover gave up the 318-foot USS *Mayflower*. Two years later, while *Mayflower* was laid up at the Philadelphia Navy Yard, she was damaged by fire and eventually was sold off at auction. Therefore, Hoover was reduced to using the one naval "yacht" available to him in Washington, a 50-foot converted admiral's barge from USS *Arizona*. She was an open boat, good only for day trips, painted black with the president's flag emblazoned on her bow. But there is no record of the president ever having used her.[1]

At that time the Depression also forced Texan William Dunning to sell *Sequoia II*. On March 20, 1931, the Department of Commerce bought her and converted her into an "inspection vessel" assigned to the department's Bureau of Inspection and Navigation. (In 1942, the duties of this bureau were transferred

President Hoover and his wife Lou, accompanied by a Secret Service agent, disembarking from *Sequoia* at Cape Henry, 1931. Courtesy Herbert Hoover Presidential Library/Museum.

over to the U.S. Coast Guard.) Her name was changed to just *Sequoia,* and she was brought east for patrol duty on the Chesapeake and Delaware Bays. There, she was used to enforce navigation rules, Prohibition, and the labor laws meant to provide fair working conditions for oystermen.

During Prohibition the Chesapeake was a regular conduit for boats running black-market booze up and down the East Coast. Reportedly, while on patrol, *Sequoia* often was mistaken for an innocent pleasure craft to the very unpleasant surprise of bootleggers when they tried to sell their wares to her crew. She was kept very busy in the early 1930s on the two bays with her enforcement duties, which required hundreds of inspections, but occasionally *Sequoia* was called upon for quite a different assignment.

President Hoover was familiar with Trumpy-designed yachts as he had divided some of his vacation time in Florida aboard two privately owned Trumpy yachts during the winter of 1928–29. Apparently he enjoyed these so-called "cruising houseboats" so much that when he heard the U.S. government had acquired one, he was tempted to use it.

His first call for *Sequoia* was on April 25, 1931, barely a month after she had been taken over by the Department of Commerce. President Hoover wanted her for a trip from Washington to Cape Henry, Virginia, where he was to attend a ceremony commemorating the 324th anniversary of the landing of the early colonists. A navy tug with Secret Service agents aboard escorted the yacht on that trip. It was the first time *Sequoia* had a U.S. president on board. The Hoovers liked *Sequoia* enough on that outing that, on returning, the president told Secretary of Commerce Robert P. Lamont that he would like to borrow her again "for special occasions."

The next special occasion was in the spring of 1932. President Hoover and his wife Lou loved to fish and considered *Sequoia* quite perfect for fishing holidays. By presidential request that year, the inspection vessel *Sequoia* was sent to Charleston, South Carolina, by way of the Intracoastal Waterway. Under the command of Lieutenant William Coad of the

President Hoover's Christmas card, 1932. Courtesy Herbert Hoover Presidential Library/Museum.

Bureau of Navigation, she was purportedly to do inspection work along the way. But the main reason for the trip was to embark the president and his wife at Savannah, Georgia, and take them along the waterway to Palm Beach, Florida, where the Hoovers would enjoy the yacht for parties, fishing, and some much-needed privacy.

The Hoovers again borrowed *Sequoia* in the heat of August 1932 for a fishing and cooling-off cruise on the Chesapeake Bay. Lou Hoover was keen on sports and fitness at that time and encouraged her somewhat overweight husband to exercise with a medicine ball on the top deck of *Sequoia*. For his safety, additional handrails were added to that deck, which previously had been used only by the crew to launch and recover *Sequoia*'s tenders. The Hoovers were so pleased with this relatively modest yacht, they decided to feature a photograph of her on their 1932 Christmas card.

President Hoover's final request for this inspection vessel was for use during his last Christmas in office. Thus *Sequoia* again was sent to Savannah, Georgia, where the president and his wife, along with his doctor and a few friends, embarked for a cruise southward to Palm Beach, Florida. Three Coast Guard vessels were assigned as escorts, including *Kilkenny*, which, being the largest escort vessel, had several shallow-water problems along the waterway. The Hoovers stopped at Sapelo Island, Georgia, for Christmas dinner at the home of their friend Howard Coffin. The *Miami Herald* reported that the president, while en route, spent time at his temporary desk on *Sequoia* to review problems over war debts and other government issues, as well as to sort out an accumulation of bills and telegrams. The paper further reported that because of choppy Atlantic Ocean waters, *Sequoia* had to take the slower inland passage. At the president's insistence, she cruised well after nightfall to be on schedule early the next morning for his deep-sea fishing trip with friends from Palm Beach. The day before Christmas, Lou Hoover wrote an enthusiastic and intimate letter to friends describing life aboard *Sequoia*.

THE WHITE HOUSE
WASHINGTON

December 24, 1932

My dear Mildred and Philippi:

We are having an extremely beautiful day. We left Savannah about half-past nine. Came down just the route we took nine months ago, and just after lunch came to anchor in one of the little side channels at the north of Ossabaw Island. Perhaps you remember it. It is the last big island north of St. Catherines.

The President, Justice, Senator and Mr. Sullivan have gone out to sea, fishing. Mr. Dunning, the Collector of the Port of Savannah, whom we did not meet when we were down because he was North then, is in charge of the expedition and has found a man as pilot and chief fisherman who is surely going to find sea bass and sea trout.

It is such a lovely afternoon. I have stayed on board, partly to sleep and partly to get the last mail accumulation off my hands. The Sequoia is as lovely as ever, - even lovelier. Up forward where flower baskets and vegetables were parked before, it is now railed in, covered with awning. Aft of the little boats on that top deck is also railed in, so that if some members of the party fall asleep while they are taking sun baths on that deck, no one has to watch them to be sure they don't roll into the sea!

The Kilkenny is along, but, alas, Captain McCoy is 70 years old, - whereby he had to automatically retire, - and I am sure he went over the side the last time with tears in his eyes!

Merry Christmas.

Lou Hoover describes her life aboard *Sequoia*.

Shortly after this last "borrowing" by President Hoover, *Sequoia* was moved up in status to become the official presidential yacht for President Franklin Delano Roosevelt.

Commissioned for President Franklin Delano Roosevelt, 1933–35

> The President has heard that the *Sequoia* is no longer needed by the Department of Commerce. If this information is correct, The President desires that the *Sequoia* be turned over to the Navy Department.
>
> —M. H. McIntyre,
> Secretary to the President

Soon after President Franklin D. Roosevelt's inauguration on March 4, 1933, the new president let it be known that he wanted a yacht for short cruises. The small, comfortable, and classy *Sequoia*, already government-owned, was an obvious choice for use on the Potomac River and the Chesapeake Bay. On March 15, the president's private secretary inquired about transferring *Sequoia* out of the Department of Commerce and into the navy for presidential use. But Secretary of Commerce Daniel C. Roper was very reluctant to lose *Sequoia* so soon after acquiring her. In his reply he stated "the boat is being used in valuable and important service by this department." To make his point he enclosed a description of the current employment of *Sequoia*.

However, it was no use. A week later, on March 23, the secretary of commerce

Tea being served on the open deck aft of the main salon aboard *Sequoia*. Missy LeHand, the president's personal secretary, is on FDR's left and Captain Wilson Brown, the president's naval aide, is on his right. Courtesy FDR Library.

March 17, 1933

RE. "SEQUOIA"

The SEQUOIA is employed on Chesapeake and Delaware Bays in the enforcement of the laws for the protection of life and welfare of seamen.

In 1912 there was discovered in the oyster fleet on Chesapeake Bay an almost unbelievable condition of shanghaiing, failure to pay wages, and ill-treatment of seamen. The first vessel of our patrol fleet was then purchased and the unlawful conditions mentioned were abated. It has been found however that continued supervision is necessary to maintain lawful conditions in the oyster fleet and finally the SEQUOIA was purchased for this purphse.

About the same time the rapid increase in the construction of motor vessel began. There are now 55,611 motor vessels on the waters covered by the Chespeake and Delaway Bays patrol boat SEQUOIA, the duty of which is to see that they are equipped with lifesaving devices and are properly navigated. In addition, there are 3,535 documented vessels of 2,898,916 gross tons supervised by the SEQUOIA to see that they comply with the navigation laws as to equipment, manning, and navigation.

During the last fiscal year the SEQUOIA reported 674 violations of the navigation laws for mitigation or remission of penalties and in the previous year 1,086 violations of law were reported in the same waters. During this period 10,654 vessels were boarded. All of this is exclusive of the supervision by the SEQUOIA of the seamen on the oyster dredges to see that they are paid their wages, have proper food, and quarters, and are humanely treated.

Incident to the above work, the SEQUOIA has been detailed on not more than six occasions during the past year to the use of the White House for very short fishing trips and similar purposes. The SEQUOIA has in no sense been considered an adjunct to the White House and is primarily a patrol boat.

/s/. A. J. Tyrer

Assistant Director
Navigation

Memo describing *Sequoia*'s duties in 1933.

THE SECRETARY OF COMMERCE
WASHINGTON

March 23, 1933

Honorable M. H. McIntyre,
Secretary to the President,
The White House,
Washington, D.C.

My dear Secretary:

We are very glad to transfer to the Navy Department for the personal use of the President the boat SEQUOIA, with the hope that he may be able to use it frequently and with great physical profit during this period of strain and stress.

I have instructed the Assistant Director of Navigation, Mr. Tyrer, to get in touch with Admiral Craven and ask the transfer as early as practicable.

Very sincerely,

DANIEL C. ROPER
Secretary of Commerce.

Concession: The President gets his wish.

bowed to the president's wishes and wrote a letter of concession to the White House.

The navy acted quickly, designating *Sequoia* "Auxiliary Miscellaneous, AG 23" and commissioning her on March 25, 1933, in Annapolis, Maryland. A young officer, Lieutenant Junior Grade John S. Blue, USN, the son of an admiral, became her first commanding officer. His orders were to deliver the yacht to the Washington Navy Yard and complete preparations for her use by the president of the United States. Two days after *Sequoia*'s commissioning at Annapolis, the navy tug *Tucumseh* took her in tow for the trip to Washington.

One of the earliest preparations the navy made was to install a small elevator to carry the president in his wheelchair from the main deck to the staterooms below so he would not have to negotiate the narrow staircase. At that time, before air-conditioning, *Sequoia*'s afterdeck was not enclosed with windowed panels as it was in later years; it was open to catch cooling breezes while underway, a feature much appreciated by guests.

Soon after *Sequoia* arrived at the Washington Navy Yard in March, the president must have been eager to inspect his new yacht and her crew. It is easy to imagine Roosevelt's first visit to her somewhat as Ronald Liston did in his article for *Sea Classics:*

> As the president is being driven from the White House to Southwest Washington in the black presidential limousine protected by secret service agents and with police escorts, the captain aboard *Sequoia*, in his dress-white uniform, makes a final inspection of his new command to check out the staterooms, the salons, the galley, the engine room, the decks, and the pilothouse. He finds all is shipshape.
>
> Lieutenant Junior Grade Blue then steps out on deck. As is customary before leaving a naval vessel, he exchanges salutes with the quarterdeck watch, then salutes the ensign flying at the stern and crosses on the gangway to the dock. He walks the length of the yacht checking that there are no blemishes on her freshly painted white topsides and that every line is clean and in place. Meanwhile, *Sequoia*'s crew

President Franklin D. Roosevelt in the lee of *Sequoia* greeting officers assigned to the Washington Navy Yard in 1933. Courtesy FDR Library.

stands at ease in two ranks on the dock awaiting the president's inspection. A U.S. Marine Corps band is nearby, ready to sound off.

The whine of sirens announces the approach of the motorcade. On arrival President Roosevelt is assisted from his limousine and pauses to observe the preparations made for his visit. The Navy Yard honors the commander in chief with a 21-gun salute that resounds all over the waterfront. The honor guard presents arms as ruffles and flourishes are heard, followed by "Hail to the Chief." As the band starts "The Star-Spangled Banner," the president turns towards the music and holds his hat over his heart. After the last note he turns back to admire the 104-foot gleaming white hull of *Sequoia* and the highly varnished wood of her long deck cabin and pilothouse.

The young captain, waiting at the top of the gangway, salutes, proud to receive on board the president of the United States.

On Sunday, April 23, 1933, just one month after *Sequoia* was commissioned,

A happy and relaxed President Franklin D. Roosevelt fishing from *Sequoia* in 1933. Courtesy FDR Library.

President Roosevelt invited his first important guest for a cruise on the Potomac River. That guest was J. Ramsey MacDonald, prime minister of Great Britain, who came to Washington for discussions on the Great Depression and the rising military threat of Nazi Germany.

During that summer of 1933 and on into October, President Roosevelt and his wife Eleanor usually spent one or two days of the weekends aboard *Sequoia*, often with a member of the cabinet. For instance, in May Roosevelt spent a weekend aboard with Secretary of the Treasury William H. Woodin. In July he invited Attorney General Homer Cummings aboard. On another weekend Secretary of Agriculture Henry A. Wallace was the principal guest.

Like any good host, the president tried to provide interesting diversions for his out-of-town guests. A sightseeing cruise aboard *Sequoia* was a favorite. During the visit to Washington by Crown Prince Ras Dexta Demtu of Ethiopia in July 1933, the prince and his retinue were treated to a cooling cruise on the Potomac River aboard *Sequoia*.

But more often *Sequoia* was used for presidential relaxation, sometimes in company with guests such as Vice President

John Nance Gardner, Supreme Court Justice Felix Frankfurter, and Secretary of the Interior Harold Ickes. On other occasions in 1933, the president would sail alone in *Sequoia* just to fish and keep cool. An entry in *Sequoia's* official logbook on July 23, 1933, dutifully records that "while anchored off Maryland Point, at the mouth of the Potomac River, the President of the United States caught his first fish [meaning from on board *Sequoia*], a four-inch perch."

At times with the president on board, *Sequoia* would encounter a naval ship on the Bay and the traditional twenty-one-gun salute for the president would boom out over the waters. Despite such occasional gunfire, his frequent guest and distant cousin Margaret "Daisy" Stuckley wrote in her diary that she found *Sequoia* "a delightful little boat . . . just a good size for a peaceful weekend."

When the president was invited in October 1933 to attend the installation

President Franklin and Mrs. Roosevelt greet Maryland Governor Albert C. Ritchie and Washington College President Hyram S. Brown, *far right,* at Chestertown. *Far left:* Maryland State Senator S. Scott Beck. Courtesy FDR Library.

First Lady Eleanor Roosevelt with her mail. Courtesy FDR Library.

of the new president of Washington College at Chestertown, Maryland, and to receive an honorary doctoral degree, he decided the most comfortable way to go was to sail in *Sequoia* from Annapolis to the Eastern Shore of Maryland. The day before the event he embarked with a few guests for a short cruise on the Bay. They anchored for the night near the mouth of the Chester River. The next morning, on schedule, an amphibian plane from Washington circled overhead, then landed close by *Sequoia* to deliver the president's mail and newspapers. All went smoothly as they sailed up the river to Chestertown except during the docking when, as the log records, "due to tricky winds and currents" *Sequoia* rammed into a piling. Two of her planks were stove in, but fortunately well above the waterline.

After that first busy presidential boating season, *Sequoia* was sent to the Norfolk Navy Yard in November 1933, for further improvements. She was drydocked in order to have several underwater planks replaced, and her gasoline engines and generators were replaced with more reliable diesel equipment. She also was equipped with new and better fuel tanks.

The president was back on board *Sequoia* during the summer of 1934. In June he cruised in her along the Connecticut coast of Long Island Sound from New Haven to New London and later to Hyde Park, New York.

At the end of 1934 the secretary of the navy wrote a letter to the president expressing his concern that *Sequoia,* being a wooden boat, was a potential fire hazard. He asked the president for authority to find a replacement for *Sequoia,* but the president would have none of it. He loved *Sequoia,* especially her low freeboard, which was so convenient for fishing. FDR immediately responded with the memorandum shown on the facing page.

Sequoia was again available for presidential use at the Washington Navy Yard by April 1935. Roosevelt sailed in her on weekends in April, May, and June. Typically, he cruised down the Potomac River with a few guests for an overnight stay at some quiet harbor. At other times he would embark at Annapolis and head for Sharps Island or Tangier Island in the

THE WHITE HOUSE
WASHINGTON

December 31, 1934.

MEMORANDUM FOR

THE SECRETARY OF THE NAVY

That is very sweet of you to think about possible danger on the SEQUOIA. Nevertheless, she is really ideal in many ways -- not too big - low free-board - good places to fish from aft, etc.

In regard to the fire hazard, I do not think it wise, in view of the constant watch being kept through the night when people are below. Therefore, I think we had better not do anything about a substitute.

F. D. R.

FDR's opinion of *Sequoia*.

Chesapeake Bay, two of his favorite fishing spots. He particularly liked fishing off Sharps Island. Apparently he considered it a lucky spot.

On these fishing trips *Sequoia*'s log showed that guests were aboard, such as Harry Hopkins, Joseph Kennedy, Ethel Du Pont, and Jack Warner. Whenever the president was aboard *Sequoia,* the U.S. Coast Guard cutter *Cuyahoga* was always in close company for backup and to provide security. That 125-foot steel vessel had been launched in 1927 and was manned by three officers and seventeen men.

A typical presidential weekend recorded in *Sequoia*'s logbook was on May 18, 1935. The log reports that *Sequoia*'s commander received his orders from the naval aide at the White House to embark the president and his guests at the Quantico Marine Base in Virginia. The log listed the guests as Colonel Edwin "Pa" Watson, the president's appointments secretary, and his wife; Samuel Rosenman, the president's speechwriter and his wife; Miss Marguerite "Missy" LeHand, the president's personal secretary; and Captain Wilson Brown, the president's naval aide. Also listed were a chief pharmacist's mate and two Secret Service agents.

That weekend the president required *Sequoia* to sail to the Honga River on the eastern side of the Bay opposite the mouth of the Patuxent River. She anchored there on Saturday night with *Cuyahoga* discreetly nearby. Early Sunday morning *Sequoia* moved up the Honga River to Crab Point for a full day of fishing. *Sequoia*'s logbook also noted that "at 1209 Coast Guard amphibian plane number 130 arrived with Secretary of the Treasury Morgenthau, Mrs. Roosevelt, and Mrs. Rhodes." The log also records that in late afternoon, *Sequoia* steamed at ten knots to Annapolis where the president and his guests disembarked.

Apparently *Sequoia* remained at Annapolis that week. The log entry for the next Saturday states: "1233 Naval Academy fired twenty-one-gun salute for President of the United States. 1233 Broke President's flag on Sequoia. 1300 Underway. . . . standing up Severn River for race course. 1320 moored to buoy at race course. 1432 Mrs. Roosevelt, Admiral and Mrs. Grayson came aboard."

Crew signaling from *Sequoia* to escort *Cuyahoga*. Coutesy © the Mariners' Museum, Newport News, Virginia.

In June 1935 Roosevelt required *Sequoia* to be in New London, Connecticut, where from her decks he and Mrs. Roosevelt could watch their son John, a member of the Harvard crew, race against Yale on the Thames River. On such occasions, for convenience and privacy, the president and Mrs. Roosevelt spent the night aboard the yacht.

During the fall of 1935 the president continued to enjoy *Sequoia*. He sailed to the Rappahannock River in Virginia for a visit to Fredericksburg. Later he was aboard for a return trip to Washington from Yorktown, Virginia. His last trip in *Sequoia* was made on October 24, 1935, when he sailed from Annapolis over to Cambridge, Maryland, to meet with Maryland's Governor Harry Nice. By then, President Roosevelt had logged thirty-six cruises aboard *Sequoia*.

Transitions

Sequoia was decommissioned on December 9, 1935, and put into a category called "in service" as the secretary of the navy's yacht. Four months later, the USS *Potomac,* a low-slung steel-hulled former Coast Guard cutter, 61 feet longer than *Sequoia* and with oceangoing capability, became the new presidential yacht.

Potomac served as President Roosevelt's yacht for the next nine years, but by 1941 she too was restricted to protected waters because structural additions to her upper decks had raised her center of gravity and reduced her stability, thus making her "cranky." *Potomac* was decommissioned on November 18, 1945, and replaced that same month by USS *Williamsburg* which became the official presidential yacht for Harry S. Truman.

CHAPTER FOUR

Secretary of the Navy's Yacht, 1936–68

> *The Prime Minister of Great Britain, the Prime Minister of Canada, and I were greatly pleased with our cruise on the USS* Sequoia.
>
> —Harry S. Truman

When *Sequoia* became the secretary of the navy's yacht, she was moved to a dock at the mouth of the Anacostia River that was a facility of the Anacostia Naval Air Station. Although she was overshadowed in size and prestige by *Potomac* and later by *Williamsburg*, she was often used by the navy secretary and his senior staff for business and recreational trips on the Potomac River.

A Special Meeting Place for President Truman

The only record in the Truman Library showing that President Harry S. Truman used *Sequoia* was when Truman took British Prime Minister Clement Attlee, Canadian Prime Minister Mackensie King, and U.S. Secretary of State James Byrnes aboard during their summit conference on Armistice Day, November 11, 1945, just before *Williamsburg* was available.

Only three months prior to that meeting on August 14, 1945, Japan had surrendered. By September, U.S. troops were replacing the Japanese occupation forces in China and South Korea and the "Truman Doctrine" was being formulated at the White House to provide aid to countries threatened by communism.

Among the postwar problems, the control of atomic weapons was a major concern of the three allied leaders who had collaborated during the war to develop the atomic bomb. During this, their first postwar conference on nuclear, technological, and scientific exchanges, they met aboard *Sequoia* for discussions on how mankind could benefit from the new science without necessarily revealing the secrets of weapon technology.

After borrowing *Sequoia* during this conference, Truman sent Secretary of the Navy James Forrestal this "bread-and-butter" note:

> The White House
> November 13, 1945
> My Dear Mr. Secretary:
> The Prime Minister of Great Britain, the Prime Minister of Canada, and I were greatly pleased with our cruise on the USS *SEQUOIA* on Armistice Day and I wish to thank you on their behalf, as well as on my own, for having placed the *SEQUOIA* at my service. The crew was efficient and most courteous and my guests and I were made very comfortable.
>
> Sincerely yours,
> s/Harry S. Truman

There is only hearsay evidence of off-the-record visits to *Sequoia* by President Truman. Rear Admiral Donald J. McDonald had this to say about keeping records in his oral-history statement filed at the U.S. Naval Institute:

> By being "In service" rather than "In commission," and by having an officer-in-charge instead of a commanding officer, an official logbook did not have to be kept and they did not have to comply with all Navy Regulations. There are advantages to having a ship that is noncommissioned versus a commissioned ship.

In *Sequoia's* case, one of those advantages surely was the ability to serve liquor on board. Also, formal records were not required to be kept of her operations or of her guests. Thus, very little solid evidence exists to document when and how often President Truman went aboard her. According to crew members at the time, the president occasionally entertained on board. It is well known that President Truman liked to play poker with his cronies, and he might have enjoyed some unrecorded poker games in the intimacy of *Sequoia* with friends such as Harry Hopkins and Vice President Alben Barkley. Truman also loved to play the piano, and it is said he had one installed in 1947 aboard *Sequoia*. Petty Officer Arthur Rollins, in the crew at the time, recalled the following: "When the president ordered the piano and a poker table, the crew had to search hard, but eventually found a small upright piano that just

On *Sequoia's* afterdeck, President Harry S. Truman sits with British Prime Minister Clement Attlee on his left and Secretary of State James Byrnes on his right. Courtesy AP Worldwide Photos.

Sequoia's officers and men in 1945 under the command of Commander J. W. Payne, Jr. Courtesy U.S. Navy.

fitted into the limited space available. The president played it, but he seemed disappointed that it had only sixty-six keys instead of the normal eighty-eight. I remember well Truman playing that piano, but I never heard him play the 'Missouri Waltz,' as everyone might think," Rollins said.

As the secretary of the navy's yacht, or just "the navy's yacht," as she was more commonly known during the Truman administration, *Sequoia* was the scene of delicate political meetings hosted on board by Secretary of the Navy James Forrestal. For instance, on August 27, 1946, Forrestal noted that he gave a dinner aboard *Sequoia* to again discuss with key advisors strategy for the unification of the armed forces. The specific purpose of that meeting, he said, was "to find out whether the Army would agree that President Truman, by executive order, should put into effect the many already agreed-upon points in the unification plan and leave the more controverted issues to Congress."[1]

Forrestal's diary records that on June 25, 1947, Senators Leverett Saltonstall and Walter F. George were his supper guests aboard *Sequoia,* this time to discuss congressional relations with the president. At that time President Truman was having difficulty convincing Congress to unify the armed forces under a single department of defense, and he sought all the congressional votes he could muster. Forrestal wrote of that evening on board *Sequoia:* "Senator George repeated his warm personal feelings towards the president and expressed regret that there was so little consultation between the president and some of his old associates in the Senate. He thought some of the opposition to the president was unnecessary."

Secretary of the Navy Forrestal's files in the National Archives provide some insight on how *Sequoia* was regarded and employed during the late 1940s. The following is a selection of notes from those files:

- In August 1945 it was decided for pay purposes, duty aboard *Sequoia* would be considered "sea duty."
- In January 1946, *Sequoia* was sent to Palm Beach, Florida, for Secretary and Mrs. Forrestal. Afterwards Forrestal sent a note to a Mr. J. S. Phipps, Esq., of Palm Beach, thanking him for the use of his boathouse on Lake Worth for docking *Sequoia.*
- In May 1946, a special White House telephone line was installed in *Sequoia.*
- On November 10, 1946, Chief Justice Fred M. Vinson used *Sequoia.* Lieutenant Commander Clark Clifford, USNR, was aboard. He was then an Assistant Naval Aide to President Truman.
- The crew of *Sequoia* in 1947 consisted of twenty-five men including the captain, two chiefs (a motor machinist's mate and boatswain's mate), four first-class petty officers (one quartermaster, two motor machinist's mates, and one electrician's mate), seven seamen, one coxswain, five stewards, and five cooks.
- On July 1, 1947, the Secretary of the Navy gave a [7:00 P.M.] dinner aboard *Sequoia* in honor of Mr. Deupress, retiring chairman of the Army and Navy Munitions Board, with President Truman and twenty-one others present, including General Eisenhower, Admiral Nimitz, and Defense Secretary Patterson.
- A memo on *Sequoia's* operations for July 1947, listed as users: July 18, General Eisenhower; July 19, Secretary of the Navy; July 22, Secretary of the Navy; July 27, Secretary of Defense.
- On June 12, 1947, Rep. Lyndon B. Johnson was aboard for a stag party given by Forrestal for politicians and navy brass including Admiral Spruance.
- On July 11, 1947, thirteen freshmen senators were invited to dinner on board. That group included Senator Joseph McCarthy of Wisconsin.

Former skipper John Besson, Jr. (later rear admiral), recalls taking the Secretary of the Navy and Mrs. Knox in *Sequoia* to Yorktown, Virginia, in 1943. Mrs. Knox was en route to Newport News to christen the carrier USS *Hornet.*

Lieutenant Commander R. Kent Rosemont (later captain), who commanded *Sequoia* for the secretary of the navy during two years late in the Truman administration, kept a record of the guests who came aboard during his tour between 1951 and 1952, and he said they added up to more than one thousand.

The Eisenhower Years, 1953–61

President Dwight D. Eisenhower's first visit to *Sequoia* was not as president, but when he was army chief of staff. On September 16, 1946, he was aboard for a two-and-a-half-hour luncheon cruise on the Potomac River with Field Marshall Bernard Montgomery of Great Britain and U.S. Chief of Naval Operations Admiral Chester Nimitz. He was again on board on July 1 and July 18, 1947, according to *The Forrestal Diaries*. The Eisenhower Presidential Library has no record of President Eisenhower ("Ike") using *Sequoia* while he was in the White House.

When Ike became president in 1953 after his landslide victory, the stately presidential yacht USS *Williamsburg* was docked at the Navy Yard and readily available for him, just as she had been for Truman.

This large yacht of 244 feet was more awkward to maneuver than her two immediate predecessors, particularly when navigating the upper tidal Potomac River, with its restricted waters and low bridges. She had not been popular with President Truman for sea trips because, as one former crew member described her, once she got to sea and encountered swells, "she bucked and rolled like a wild bull." But in quiet waters Truman used her for entertaining his official visitors and for the occasional poker game with his cronies.

Shortly after President Eisenhower came into office, he dispensed with *Williamsburg* for reasons of economy and his aversion to yachts in general. After only one trip aboard *Williamsburg*, Ike decided to have her sold. Archivist Herbert L. Pankratz at the Eisenhower Library wrote, "Ike felt that yachts were too opulent a symbol for an American president to be associated with."[2]

However, the commander of *Sequoia* in 1953, Lieutenant R. A. "Chic" Bowling (later captain), reported an event that took place on board the yacht during his watch concerning national security. He said Eisenhower had campaigned on a promise for a "new look" to the national defense policy—one that depended not only on large standing forces, but also on the threat of massive retaliation with nuclear weapons. In July, a few months after he came into office, Ike asked his four chiefs of staff to work on his new defense policy. But there were concerns about where they could best do their classified work without disrupting the normal operation of the joint staff and without attracting unwelcome attention by the media.

In August of 1953 Eisenhower asked to borrow *Sequoia* from the secretary of the navy for this purpose, so the four four-star officers could complete their study in a secure and isolated place and produce their report.

Secure communications equipment was a primary consideration to enable two-way conversations to and from the yacht. This posed a problem, as the normal equipment was elaborate and would require more space than was available in *Sequoia*'s small cabins. After some "head scratching," Lieutenant Bowling suggested the use of the compact crypto system then installed in submarines. With the approval of the Bureau of Ships, that became the answer. A crypto system was installed that could be fitted into the small office opposite the captain's cabin. A radio operator and a specially cleared communications officer were added to the crew for temporary duty. It worked well in the tests, Bowling said, but was never needed.

Bowling described the day all that "brass" came aboard "with no honors or fanfare. Arriving were Admiral Arthur W. Radford, USN, Chairman, Joint Staff; Admiral Robert B. Carney, Chief of Naval Operations; General Matthew B. Ridgway, Army Chief of Staff; and General Nathan F. Twining, Air Force Chief of Staff. . . . During the day we cruised up and down the Potomac between the Anacostia River and Dahlgren [a naval station on the Potomac River in Virginia] and at night we anchored out. After about three days . . . we were directed to [moor at] Dahlgren . . . so the guests could go ashore to communicate by secure phone. . . . After one more night *Sequoia* returned to Anacostia where the distinguished guests disembarked."[3]

Thus, some history was made aboard *Sequoia* in 1953 when Eisenhower's joint chiefs were sequestered on board to work out the new defense policy that became known as Mutually Assured Destruction (MAD), a policy that eventually helped end the Cold War.

During the Eisenhower administration, *Sequoia* continued to be moored at the Naval Air Station on the Anacostia River not far from the Navy Yard. Although she was still designated the secretary of the navy's yacht, of course she was available for presidential use. *Sequoia*'s next skipper, Lieutenant William Meanix, said, "We tried hard through President Eisenhower's staff to get him to use *Sequoia,* but the answer always came back that there was no way he was going to risk the unfavorable publicity of being seen on the yacht *Sequoia* after having done away with the yacht *Williamsburg.*" However, Mrs. Eisenhower was aboard *Sequoia* at least twice. "One time, she was the guest of honor of several cabinet wives," Meanix recalls, "and I had to search all over town to get her favorite bourbon [Barclay's] on board, but she partook of very little of it and afterwards she was extremely gracious in shaking hands and thanking every member of my crew."

At that time much of *Sequoia*'s upper deck was taken up with boats. *Sequoia* was described by the Navy Department in 1954 as having on board for auxiliary purposes four small craft: a 21-foot Chris-Craft motorboat and a 14-foot V-bottom craft, plus a dinghy and a 14-foot skiff, both powered by outboard motors. It was customary every January for *Sequoia* to be hauled out on the ways at the Navy

Yard for work on her hull, and at that time all her cleats and chocks were removed for new chrome plating to be done at the Gun Factory.

On the night of October 16, 1954, hurricane Hazel blew through Washington, D.C., putting *Sequoia* at some risk. Crew member Willis Boyd, a boatswain's mate at the time, remembers that night well.

> The forecasters had predicted very strong winds and tides eight feet above normal with high tide at about 2200. In the early evening we got the interesting news that we would be getting underway around 2100. By that time the winds were at forty knots and the tide was over our dock by three feet so we had to cut our lines. One of the seamen took a fire ax to do the job. The wind blew us off the naval station dock, and we headed east on the Anacostia River to get to the other side of the South Capital Street Bridge where the waters are more protected. But before we got to the bridge the captain said we would have to turn around as there would not be enough maneuvering room on the other side. We turned westward. "Head straight into the wind" was the order. Several times we cruised back and forth over the short distance between the bridge and the naval station, but each time we turned, the wind [reported to have gusted up to ninety-eight miles per hour that night] would hit us broadside and make us list 15 degrees. I wondered if I was going for a swim that night.
>
> The captain ordered us to put on life jackets; then I knew it was serious. After the third turn the captain said he was going to anchor in the lee of a building he thought might give us protection from the wind. We dropped anchor and let out ten fathoms of chain. After about two minutes with the chain taut we began to drag anchor. The captain ordered the other anchor dropped. [One can imagine the tension in the pilothouse was then about equal to the tension on the anchor chains.] At that point the supply officer, a friend also from Kentucky, leaned over and whispered "If we get those two anchor chains twisted we *are* in trouble."
>
> The captain, aware of the potential danger, soon ordered both anchors up. We resumed cruising the river in long elliptical circles until daybreak. By morning the tide had ebbed and we could see our dock again. We moored at 0800 and things looked pretty good considering all the wind and rain. The captain gave us the day off, but the following day we had the big job of cleaning, sanding, and painting the two anchors and every link of their chains.[4]

Eisenhower's Secretary of Defense Neil McElroy invited Lord Louis Mountbatten, chief of the British Defense Staff, to Washington in August 1959. At that time the Soviet "Sputnik" and the so-called "missile gap" were defense concerns. Presumably the men discussed the military implications of the Soviet advances. Afterward McElroy sequestered *Sequoia* for a formal dinner cruise that honored Lord and Lady Mountbatten.

Sequoia had a first-class navy cook, Fausto Pagal, who received some publicity. He enjoyed his fifteen minutes of fame when his photo and several of his recipes were published in the *Washington Star*. They included such treats as his Sequoia Brownies, Orange Cookies, Sequoia Dressing, and Chicken Crepes.

The *Washington Star* described *Sequoia*'s master suite at this time as furnished in French Provincial with a green carpet and green and white curtains. The article also described the rattan furniture in the after salon as covered with an attractive green and blue print on a gold background.

Naval Administrative Unit, 1953–77

Shortly after President Eisenhower ordered *Williamsburg* to be decommissioned as the presidential yacht in 1953, an organization called the Naval Administrative Unit was formed at the Washington Navy Yard. It probably had such an innocuous name so as not to attract undue attention on the Hill when it was being funded. The purpose of the new unit was to provide boating and other support services for the president's official and personal requirements. The use of *Sequoia* would be part of these services, although she was designated the secretary of the navy's yacht. This new unit was a curious command as it had to be responsive to both the White House and the Navy Department.

Typically the unit consisted of 2 officers and about 120 enlisted men, including a Coast Guard detachment. The commanding officer, usually a lieutenant commander, was also officer-in-charge of *Sequoia*. He was authorized to wear the "Presidential Service Badge" and was considered part of the White House staff, reporting directly to the president's military assistant.

The Naval Administrative Unit's executive officer, usually a lieutenant, could expect to move up to officer-in-charge after two years. The unit consisted of not only *Sequoia*'s crew and the crew for several smaller craft, but also other enlisted personnel who provided services at the White House and at Camp David. The unit's officers were usually bachelors because the assignment sometimes required them to be escorts for single ladies at the White House.

The unit's enlisted complement consisted of men of considerable and varied skills, including stewards, electricians, mechanics, carpenters, sailmakers, cooks, boatswains, and yeomen, to name but a few. They were a handy group with all the skills needed to provide technical support for *Sequoia* and the other small craft, such as repairing engines, handling haul-outs and replanking, making awnings, and even reupholstering chairs. Twenty-six of these men were assigned specifically to *Sequoia*. They were responsible for keeping the secretary of the navy's yacht painted and polished and ready to go at any time with full catering service for guests. For operations, one commissioned officer, three chiefs, six seamen, one cook, and fifteen stewards were readily available.

However, instead of using *Sequoia*, President Eisenhower favored the two smaller recreational boats also in the care of the Naval Administrative Unit. At his request they were refurbished at a reported cost of half a million dollars, and he renamed them after his two granddaughters. The 92-foot *Lenore* became *Barbara Anne,* and the 64-foot *Margie* became *Susie E.* (for Susan Elaine). The president always referred to these two boats as "cruisers," never as "yachts." Following his style, so did everyone else.

According to crew member John Susa, who was assigned to *Sequoia* between 1953 and 1956, "*Sequoia* was used by undersecretaries and assistant secretaries of the Defense Department for a cruise nearly every night, but usually we got back to the dock by ten o'clock." When Nixon was Eisenhower's vice president, "He came aboard *Sequoia,*" said Susa, "and sometimes came down to the engine room to drink coffee with the crew. The vice president told us he didn't much like the coffee up in the salon, but I think he wanted to be like one of us." Dix Darby, *Sequoia*'s chief engineer from 1959 through 1961, noted "we were instructed to initiate no conversations with guests, but if a guest wanted to talk to you, you stayed as long as they wanted."

Sequoia was used by senior government officials in the 1950s often more than twice a week, former Quartermaster Jim Davis said. "On many weekends we would take guests for an overnight anchorage as far as Cobb Island on the lower Potomac, or sometimes to Popes Creek [just north of the route 301 bridge where it crosses the Potomac]. The crew

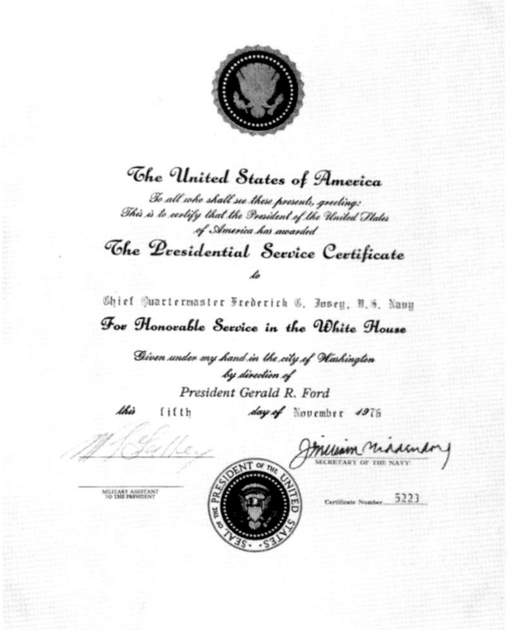

The United States of America
To all who shall see these presents, greeting:
This is to certify that the President of the United States of America has awarded
The Presidential Service Certificate
to
Chief Quartermaster Frederick C. Josey, U.S. Navy
For Honorable Service in the White House
Given under my hand in the city of Washington
by direction of
President Gerald R. Ford
this fifth day of November 1976

MILITARY ASSISTANT TO THE PRESIDENT

SECRETARY OF THE NAVY

SEAL OF THE PRESIDENT OF THE UNITED STATES

Certificate Number 5223

The Presidential Service Badge and certificate are authorized after one year of presidential service. The badge, *below,* is worn on the left pocket of the naval uniform. Courtesy Andrew Combe.

was never allowed to take photographs during those trips. At that time *Sequoia* carried a 14-foot varnished Chris-Craft runabout in davits on the port side which was very popular with guests. Sometimes with no guests aboard we could make an overnight cruise down river just for the crew's recreation and all hands could go swimming."

During the 1950s *Sequoia* had regular overhauls at the Trumpy yard in Annapolis. The budget for her annual maintenance then was about $150,000. During those years a gyrocompass was installed in the forepeak with gyro repeaters placed on deck for taking bearings; one stood on each side of the pilothouse. Also, new engine controls were installed in the pilothouse.

When Kennedy succeeded Eisenhower in the White House, the names of the so-called "cruisers" of the Naval Administrative Unit were again changed by presidential request. *Barbara Anne* became *Honey Fitz* in honor of Kennedy's grandfather, and *Susie E.* became *Patrick J.* in honor of Kennedy's young nephew. Still later, during Nixon's administration, *Honey Fitz* was renamed *Patricia,* and *Patrick J.* was renamed *Julie,* to honor the president's daughters. But after relatively light use by Presidents Johnson and Nixon, these two boats were sold off in July 1970. After that the only vessel the Naval Administrative Unit had to look after was *Sequoia.*

At times there was some misunderstanding in the navy about the Naval Administrative Unit. For instance, during the Nixon administration in 1973, the *Washington Post* reported that a couple of members of the Naval Administrative Unit had been disciplined for smoking marijuana while off duty. When that report came to the attention of the chief of naval personnel, he called in Lieutenant Commander Andrew Combe, the officer-in-charge of the unit at the time, to ask why the matter had not come to his attention through the normal chain of command. Combe said, "I had to tell him the reason was because there is no direct chain of command between *Sequoia* and navy headquarters. I explained to the admiral that I reported directly to the president's military aide and through him to the president."

While Nixon was president, "*Sequoia* was kept at the Washington Navy Yard in a compound surrounded by an eight-foot cinder-block wall electrically wired for security." Combe said. "A high sentry tower from which the compound could be monitored was manned around the clock and augmented by a roving marine security guard. Thus, security was very tight. All personnel were thoroughly vetted before being assigned to *Sequoia.* Nevertheless, when the president was aboard, the Secret Service would not allow the crew to carry sidearms.

"The duty crew for *Sequoia* was usually on twenty-minute standby. With President Nixon aboard, we got underway with a crew usually of ten men and two officers, plus four Secret Service agents. The yacht was always escorted by two fast Coast Guard boats, each carrying Secret Service agents. Only one boat escorted *Sequoia* when the president was not aboard. One of the speedboats, code named 'Rockfish,' was designated to take the president ashore in a hurry if necessary."

When *Sequoia* made her way down the Potomac River with the president on board, a limousine and escort cars would

Members of the Naval Administrative Unit assigned to care for *Sequoia* in 1966. Courtesy U.S. Navy.

follow along on a road close to the river and keep in radio contact with the yacht. In case of an emergency—or if the president just wanted to avoid any press waiting at the Navy Yard for his return—a small boat could ferry him to shore.

"Keeping *Sequoia's* bar well stocked was one of my unusual duties," said Combe. "For that particular purpose, I had a government charge account at Washington's Central Liquor Store. The Administrative Unit's account was part of the Naval District's budget; therefore I was never short of funds for the president's yacht."

Boatswain's Mate Ken Ruse, recalling the spirit of those times when he was a member of the crew from 1973 to 1976, said: "*Sequoia's* crew was a tight little group. We not only worked together well, but we played together well. We played lots of volleyball, and about twice a month we'd go on a picnic. The first job for any boatswain's mate newly assigned to the Administrative Unit was to paint the curb white on the dock along where *Sequoia* tied up. Only after that assignment and other menial jobs did he become a true crew member. Two guys were assigned to maintain the yacht's topsides, particularly the waterline which they had to scrub every day. When they needed to repaint the waterline, we filled several fifty-gallon trash cans with water and hung them over one side to create a list so they could paint along the side that was raised. We repainted the hull as needed during the summer and again when she was hauled out every year. One year I remember we replaced about forty of her twenty-foot hull planks."

The Naval Administrative Unit ceased to exist in 1977 after *Sequoia* was sold.

Kennedy and *Sequoia*, 1961–63

When John F. Kennedy (JFK) came to the White House with his glamorous wife Jackie in 1961, it was the beginning of a new age known for its youth and idealism and for the start of a long economic boom. Some people called it "the Camelot Years." In Europe, the Berlin Wall— which became a symbol of the Cold War— was erected to prevent East Germans from fleeing to a better life in the West.

During Kennedy's administration, *Sequoia* continued as the secretary of the navy's yacht. She was usually moored at the Naval Air Station near the mouth of the Anacostia River with a crew of one officer and twenty-three enlisted men, including eight stewards. There was no presidential yacht per se at the time, but two smaller navy boats were still available at the Navy Yard for senior government officials. Most often, President Kennedy used the 92-foot boat *Honey Fitz* that earlier had borne the names *Lenore* and *Barbara Anne*. (After this yacht was sold into private hands in 1970, she was renamed *The Presidents* and was put into charter service.)

When the president of Pakistan visited Washington in July 1961, a grand state dinner was arranged in his honor, not at the White House as was customary, but for the first time at Mt. Vernon. In true Kennedy style, the 130 guests were sailed to Mt. Vernon aboard *Sequoia* and *Honey Fitz*. The guests of honor, President Ayub Khan and his attractive daughter Begum Nasir Auvangzeb, sailed aboard *Sequoia*. A trio from Lester Lannon's band serenaded them during the hour-and-a-half cruise to the landing at Mt. Vernon. Meanwhile, the president and Jackie were driven down by limousine to greet their guests when they arrived.

Only two occasions of the president being on board *Sequoia* are recorded at the Kennedy Library. First was the celebration of his last birthday, his forty-sixth. That party was held the evening of May 29, 1963. The host was the president's good friend Paul "Red" Fay, whom he had appointed as undersecretary of the navy. The merry gathering of twenty-seven included Jackie Kennedy, Edward and Robert Kennedy with their wives, actor David Niven and his wife, artist Bill Walton, journalist Charles Bartlett and his wife, Senator George Smathers and his wife, Pat Kennedy Lawford, *Washington Post* Editor Ben Bradlee and his

After arriving at Mt. Vernon aboard *Sequoia,* the president of Pakistan and his daughter were welcomed by the Kennedys. Before the state dinner, they posed for photographers on the front steps. Secretary of State Dean Rusk is seen at left. Courtesy Abbie Rowe, National Park Service/John Fitzgerald Kennedy Library, Boston.

wife (who had been close neighbors of the Kennedys), artist Mary Meyer, PT-boat sailor James Reed, sister Eunice Kennedy Shriver and her husband, old friend and Broadway producer Charles Spalding, former prep-school classmate Lemoyne Billings, Enud Sztanko, and "Fifie" Cushing. Three musicians were somehow squeezed into the festive main salon to serenade the party.

The menu for the evening included the following:

Appetizer: Crabmeat Ravigote
Entree: Roast Filet of Beef, Noodle Casserole, Asparagus Hollandaise
Dessert: Bombe President, Sauce Chocolate
Champagne: Cuvée Dom Perignon 1955

Afterwards, the president, seated in a rocking chair in the aft salon, opened his presents. It was a very happy and carefree occasion (some called it "wild") despite threatening thunderstorms and steamy weather on the Potomac River. Rumors to the contrary, Marilyn Monroe was not

The president responding to a birthday toast in the main salon of *Sequoia.* Courtesy Robert L. Knudsen, White House/John Fitzgerald Kennedy Library, Boston.

there to sing "Happy Birthday," but Undersecretary of the Navy Paul Fay did sing for the president a favorite song called "Me and My Shadow." The party lasted until well after midnight.[5]

According to the president's appointment books, the other occasion when the president was on board *Sequoia* was for a Potomac River cruise on July 8, 1963, but no details are given about that cruise other than that he was again a guest of Paul Fay.

However, former crew members claim that Kennedy was aboard *Sequoia* on several other occasions. Once the president sailed to Annapolis aboard the yacht to attend a navy football game.

Seaman Ralph Bolin described the first time President Kennedy visited *Sequoia* in 1961. "One weekend President and Mrs. Kennedy came to the Navy Yard to go aboard *Honey Fitz.* As they walked past *Sequoia* the president did a double take and asked the crew, 'Whose boat is this?'

"'The secretary of the navy's, sir,' responded the petty officer in charge of the crew that had come to attention on the dock. *Sequoia* happened to be there to pick up guests of the secretary of the navy, but was regularly docked around the bend of the Anacostia River at the Naval Station. The president and Jackie boarded together and after inspecting all over the yacht they declared they should be using her."

Boatswain's Mate Bill Austin claimed that at a later time when the president and Jackie were aboard for a weekend cruise to St. Mary's, Maryland, "A hell of a storm came up at night and the runabout tied up astern broke loose. To find and recover it in the dark required the searchlight, but the yacht had to be turned to enable the light to bear on the drifting runabout. The captain hesitated to start the *Sequoia*'s engines and maneuver for fear of disturbing the sleeping president. However, Kennedy heard the efforts being made to recover the boat. He came on deck and immediately upon understanding the situation urged the captain to maneuver the yacht as necessary." However, Arthur Ismay (who was in command at the time) says this story is more likely about the secretary of the navy, whom he recalls was aboard that night, not the president.

Austin also said: "Kennedy became tight with the crew. He bought a speedboat and had it installed on board *Sequoia,* then told the crew they could use it. He liked to visit the crew's quarters and chat with us. We had a small black-and-white TV at the time which he replaced with a large color TV." Austin said at least three other Kennedy dinner parties were held on board. Rumors were circulated suggesting that Kennedy held some "hot parties" aboard *Sequoia,* although Arthur Ismay insists there were none.

Crew member Bolin said that when senior government officials used *Sequoia,* he and the rest of the crew were always ordered to remain in the crew's quarters when not required on deck. However, the crew was required to go on deck every forty-five minutes to drain the air-conditioning system, and they could see out of the corner of their eyes what was going on. Bolin recalled some rowdy parties on board, but not when the president was there. After such parties, he said, the first job of the crew early on the morning after was to go through the cabins and remove all clues of the evening's festivities.

Bolin also recalled a time when *Sequoia* was underway with the Kennedy family, and the Kennedy children invaded the crew's quarters. "You are not allowed down here," the crew told them.

"We can go wherever we want," came the reply.

"Okay, you can come down here, but only if you bring us some of the dessert," a crew member said jokingly.

Caroline and the others soon returned with the remains of dessert—half a cake. The crew exclaimed, "Wow, we just wanted a taste, not the rest of the cake."

"We can't take it back now!" Caroline said.

The crew proceeded to eat the entire leftover cake. "Then we dropped the cake pan overboard to hide the evidence which created a small mystery among the stewards over their missing cake pan," Bolin said.

The crew enjoyed an example of the president's sense of humor too. According to Boatswain's Mate Austin, "When I was newly on board *Sequoia* one of my

The president opened presents in the aft salon. He holds a picture of himself at a young age with his dog. In the left foreground are David Niven and K. LeMoyne Billings. *Left to right:* Sargent Shriver, Ted Kennedy, JFK, Jackie, Eunice Shriver, and Senator George Smathers and Rosemary Smathers. Courtesy Robert L. Knudsen, White House/John Fitzgerald Kennedy Library, Boston.

jobs was to pipe the president aboard. The president, being an ex-navy man, knew the piping was supposed to start when he stepped on the brow [ramp] and stop when he arrived on board. So Kennedy teased me. The president stepped onto the brow and I began piping, then he backed off and I stopped piping. Then he got back on the brow, and I started piping again, but then the president went only halfway up and stood there waiting for me to run out of breath. Then, laughing, the president said to me, 'Nice job, Boats.'"

Lieutenant Commander Ismay, then a bachelor, lived on board during the summer months, bunking on the lower deck in the small single cabin on the starboard side. His crew lived ashore except for the duty crew, who slept in the forecastle. Ismay met his wife-to-be while he was in command of *Sequoia.* He believes she first fell in love with the yacht and later with him.

During the Kennedy administration, members of Congress and the press apparently became suspicious over who used *Sequoia* and for what purpose. Captain Alex A. Kerr, who at the time was on the staff of Secretary of the Navy Fred Korth, recalled in the oral history series of the Naval Institute:

> One or more members of Congress requested that the log of *Sequoia* be examined to see who the guests were with a view to showing that Korth was using government facilities to further his private business. I had the [informal] log in my possession. I got it from *Sequoia* to look at it when people in Congress began talking about looking at the log.
>
> The log of *Sequoia* is a very sensitive document, because *Sequoia* was not only used by the secretary of the navy, but it was used by many, many other people in government, often to meet with people under circumstances that would be impossible at their own offices. For instance, if Secretary of State Dean Rusk wanted to have the Saudi ambassador and Israeli ambassador at the same time for discussions, the proper place was aboard *Sequoia*. This is the kind of thing that went on. Many of the top people in government had had meetings aboard *Sequoia* which they wanted to be entirely private and not available to the press for very good reasons . . . [thus] the log was never made public. Executive privilege was invoked by President Kennedy."[6]

Shortly after Kennedy's assassination, Arthur Ismay was called by a navy lawyer and ordered to destroy any "personal logs" he might have kept with names of the guests who came aboard during his watch. He complied with that order by having a fire built in an oil drum, and he now says regretfully, "That's where it went."

President Johnson at lunch with unidentified ambassador on *Sequoia*'s upper deck. Courtesy LBJ Library, photo by Yoichi Okamoto.

CHAPTER FIVE

Again the President's Yacht, 1968–77

I loved the Sequoia . . . *So many memories come to mind of the times my family spent aboard this grand vessel.*
—Lady Bird Johnson, 1987

When *Hello Dolly* was a hit on Broadway, it was also the time when President Lyndon Baines Johnson committed U.S. troops to combat in Vietnam, and when he initiated his civil rights legislation and his Great Society program resulting in new environmental, educational, and health care legislation.

Johnson and *Sequoia*

After Johnson came to the White House in 1963, he seemed reluctant to use *Sequoia.* She was still the secretary of the navy's yacht, but of course, she was also available to the president. Possibly his reluctance was because of the yacht's association with his murdered predecessor. *Honey Fitz* and *Patrick J.,* the two smaller cabin cruisers, were also available to him at the Washington Navy Yard, but he probably felt they were a bit small for his Texan style. He had received a report from his staff that *Honey Fitz* could seat only eight persons for a dinner party, and *Patrick J.* was unsuitable for any dinner party.

However, after being elected for a full term in 1964, Johnson began to take more interest in the 104-foot secretary of the navy's yacht, then moored at the Anacostia Naval Station, and he occasionally borrowed her.

Sequoia had seen relatively light presidential use during the Truman, Eisenhower, and Kennedy years, but Johnson realized that the yacht would be an excellent place to lobby for his programs. She would also provide a convenient retreat and diversion from his worries over the war in Vietnam.

By July 1965 Johnson's interest in *Sequoia* had risen to the point where he requested the navy to modify *Sequoia*'s top deck so more guests could be accommodated. The Bureau of Ships issued a memorandum in August stating "The Chief

President Johnson boarding *Sequoia,* 1965. Courtesy LBJ Library, photo by Yoichi Okamoto.

Executive . . . has requested that the craft be modified to the extent that the boats, davits, and dunnage boxes [for sailors' personal gear] be removed from the top deck, and the deck be equipped with carpets and rattan furniture for additional passenger space. Improved access would be by a staircase installed at the aft end of the main lounge."[1] This alteration required the top deck to be strengthened and new stanchions and railings installed all around for safety. Former engineering crew member Bud Haviland said that at the time, *Sequoia* was powered by new 6-71 diesel engines, which had been installed during her 1965 winter layup.

These alterations were completed in January 1966 at the Trumpy yard in Annapolis and gave *Sequoia* a new look. They were followed by navy inclining experiments that determined *Sequoia* had adequate stability to accommodate forty passengers on her new top deck. The report noted that with only 3 feet of freeboard under her windows, the yacht should not be inclined to more than seventeen degrees. However, the Bureau of Ships reported to *Sequoia*'s commander that under present conditions she could safely withstand a fifty-knot beam wind.[2]

At that time, Lieutenant Thomas Morgan, newly assigned as officer-in-charge of the secretary of the navy's yacht, wrote an official "handout" about *Sequoia.* In the introduction, he stated:

> Since 1880 it has been a tradition of the U.S. Navy that a special ship be designated for the use of the Secretary of the Navy. The present ship is the USS *Sequoia* (AG23).

Morgan went on to describe his new command as follows:

> The hull . . . is constructed of fir planking and the deckhouse is constructed of teak wood. The salon is paneled with mahogany, retaining its natural red finish. The other woodwork is trimmed in brown. There are four staterooms with adjoining baths. Three have twin beds, and one was a single used by the officer-in-charge. All rooms are air-conditioned. The main salon has a buffet table which seats eighteen guests. Aft of the salon is a large glass-panel enclosed veranda which can accommodate twelve persons. For stability purposes and for safety, no more than thirty-eight guests can be accommodated aboard the ship.
>
> The USS *Sequoia* carries a 16-foot outboard motorboat with a capacity of six persons. Due to the ship's restricted stability, she is used only for inland water cruises. . . . On board there are two home-type ranges, one cold box and two chill boxes in addition to a built-in refrigerator.
>
> She is painted white with green on the overheads and decks. She has two 6-71 Gray Marine diesel engines, each rated at 225 hp. Her speed is ten knots.

The pamphlet concluded with this footnote about her crew:

> She is presently manned by a crew of twenty-three enlisted men including a force of eight stewards. The officer-in-charge is Lieutenant Thomas F. Morgan, USN, a graduate of Dartmouth College, class of 1959, and the Fletcher School of Law and Diplomacy, Tufts University, class of 1966.[3]

After Johnson announced in 1965 the increase of U.S. forces in Vietnam from 75,000 to 125,000 men, he worried how that move was being received at home and abroad. He was concerned it might jeopardize realization of his "Great Society" dream. He also felt he needed to have more foreign support. To get in closer touch with the diplomatic corps, he invited several groups of foreign ambassadors assigned to Washington to cruise with him in *Sequoia.* That gave him a captive focus group with which he could discuss his Vietnam policies and get some firsthand feedback. White House records show the following series of onboard meetings:

July 15, 1965	African ambassadors
August 25, 1965	Various foreign ambassadors
July 13, 1966	Various foreign ambassadors
July 20, 1966	African ambassadors
July 27, 1966	Ambassadors from the Far East, Near East, and South Asia

President Johnson was on board *Sequoia* the day riots broke out in Detroit in 1967. According to Dennis Cardinal, who was helmsman at the time, a call came in from J. Edgar Hoover on the red phone installed in the pilothouse. "It was

In the main salon of *Sequoia* on August 12, 1965, President Johnson is explaining his Vietnam policies to ambassadors of Great Britain, Australia, West Germany, and Nicaragua. Courtesy LBJ Library, photo by Yoichi Okamoto.

about whether to use federal troops. We heard Johnson give him the go-ahead order over the pilothouse phone."

By September 1968, Johnson wanted *Sequoia* to be turned over to the White House for control and designated as "the presidential yacht." The officer-in-charge of *Sequoia* at that time was Lieutenant Leonard Moore, USN. He remembered he had to do most of the paperwork. "Although it was the president's decision, I earned the reputation in the Pentagon as 'The person who stole the Secretary of the Navy's Yacht.'"[4]

From then on, crew members were required to have a special White House clearance to be on duty with the president on board. According to the book *American Naval Fighting Ships, Sequoia* was assigned primary employment as the presidential yacht in January 1969, but that status lasted only until June of that year when she resumed her designation as the secretary of the navy's yacht. In any case, the changes in designation seemed to have been only technical and had little practical effect on Johnson's use of the yacht.

However, Moore said that President Johnson not only appropriated the secretary of the navy's yacht and had her moved from the Anacostia Naval Station to the Navy Yard, he also demanded more changes. The president wanted larger

Texas-size doorknobs installed to better fit his big hands. He wanted more headroom in the presidential shower to accommodate his six-foot three-inch frame. The crew lowered the shower floor four inches for him. Johnson wanted to watch television from the bed in the presidential suite, so a hole was cut in the paneling to accommodate a twenty-seven-inch set. He may be responsible also for having the hinged panel installed in the door of the presidential suite to allow messages to be passed in without opening the door. Alterations were made in the wet bar where Roosevelt's elevator had been located so the liquor was more easily seen and accessible during meetings with congressmen and cronies.

Most of these changes to *Sequoia* also were done at the Trumpy yard in Annapolis. Moore said that when the yacht arrived at that yard, John Trumpy would not allow *Sequoia* to enter until the propane tanks—which had been installed in 1968 to fuel the galley stoves—were removed, as he was greatly concerned about them catching fire while his men were working on board.

With these alterations completed, Johnson used *Sequoia* even more for his "up close and personal" style, to lobby Congress in support of his Great Society program and to obtain backing for his debatable Vietnam war policies. He liked to give the impression to his guests that he would not allow the boat to return to the dock until they agreed to go along with his ideas. Crew members also noticed that when alone, the president liked to settle into a big black Lazy Boy recliner he had installed on the starboard side of the after salon and work the phone from *Sequoia*.

Sometimes the president came aboard with very little prior notice, in part for security reasons. Moore recalled more than one occasion when, after receiving a phone message from the White House saying that the president was on his way, a mad scramble took place to get all his key crew members together in proper uniform and ready to go. Once after saluting President Johnson as he arrived, Moore checked his watch and found it was only twenty minutes since he had been notified by the White House.

The president often would invite his immediate aides and sometimes a few newsmen to cruise with him. Johnson seemed to like hosting parties on board, although he is also remembered by the crew as being quite "low key" when alone, or just with Lady Bird. Crew member

The president taking calls aboard *Sequoia* in 1968. Courtesy LBJ Library, photo by Yoichi Okamoto.

Jerry Hammel said that the cook often made "baked Alaska" for the president as it was one of his favorite desserts. Another favorite was pistachio ice cream. "When we discovered there was none on board for his birthday," Mike Harreth, a seaman at the time, said, "we got some delivered by helicopter and had it lowered to us on board. There was nothing we wouldn't do for that president."

On hot summer nights Johnson liked to watch movies on board in his "skivvies," especially home movies of his ranch, recalls crew member Robert King Baer. The crew would put up a portable screen on the upper deck for him just behind the stack. Dennis Cardinal was part of the crew at the time, and he told this story. "Once, President Johnson was watching the film *Patton* on the upper deck while *Sequoia* was underway on the Potomac River. Although the cooling breeze was nice, it caused ripples across the screen that annoyed the president, so he ordered the *Sequoia* stopped in mid-channel for about an hour until the movie was over."

"Six of us lived on board," Hammel said. "We each got subsistence pay of an extra $77.10 a month for meals. We'd pool that money and eat very well. All six of us slept up forward in regular navy-type chain bunk beds. The captain also lived on board. He occupied the small single stateroom and ate separately. We called *Sequoia* 'The Lady.' All hands took her very personally like the yacht was our very own. We felt it a great honor to be in her crew."

Mrs. Johnson seldom went on board without the president but, on September 10, 1966, she and Mrs. Henry Fowler, wife of the secretary of the treasury, organized a ladies luncheon in honor of Madame Ne Win of Burma. The *Washington Post* reported that the luncheon cruise down the river included two other cabinet wives, Mrs. Dean Rusk and Mrs. Stewart Symington.[5]

Lady Bird Johnson particularly liked the traditional navy honors paid by the crew when the yacht arrived during daylight hours at George Washington's tomb at Mt. Vernon. On the approach *Sequoia* would slow, and the crew would man the rail. The ship's bell would be tolled and the ensign dipped to half mast. When opposite the tomb, the command to salute would be given and "taps" played. Guests on deck stood at attention facing Mt. Vernon and holding their hands over their hearts. After taps the tolling ceased and the ensign was two-blocked (raised). Then a tape of "The Star-Spangled Banner" would be played over the speaker system, after which "carry on" would be ordered. It was an impressive ceremony, and Lady Bird wanted all her guests to experience it.

Moore described one downriver cruise late in the afternoon with the president and first lady and their guests aboard. "Just as I was preparing to turn the yacht around for the trip back to keep to the president's schedule, I got word that Mrs. Johnson wanted to continue on to Mt. Vernon for rendering the traditional honors opposite George Washington's tomb. I protested, but Mrs. Johnson insisted, so I pushed the yacht to full speed and instructed the chief boatswain's mate to start the ceremony promptly. As we approached with the sun setting directly behind Mt. Vernon, we ran the honors ceremony. The return trip at full speed was a bit bumpy, but we made it to the yard on time. As Mrs. Johnson departed, she came up to me, 'Well, Captain, we are not late, but ten minutes early by my watch.' She then complimented me on the trip with the nicest sunset, adding 'and I want the sun just like that every time.' What could I say but, 'yes Ma'am?'"

During Johnson's tenure he frequently entertained members of Congress and their wives aboard the yacht. One such guest was Mrs. John Sherman, wife of the U.S. senator from Kentucky. At the time, she wrote a newsletter about life in the capital, and in the September 7, 1966, issue, she had this to say about *Sequoia:*

> The little yacht has many duties. She is often used for ladies luncheons . . . [to host] the wife of a visiting President or Foreign Minister. At these affairs, the brass is well polished, pennants are flying, starched-white-jacketed crew is in attendance. *[Sequoia]* steams proudly down to Mt.Vernon on the Potomac,

President Johnson talking shop with foreign ambassadors on the upper deck of *Sequoia*. Courtesy LBJ Library, photo by Yoichi Okamoto.

Aerial view of *Sequoia* moored at the Navy Yard in 1989. *Honey Fitz* is moored in the pen and *Guardian* is at the center of the photograph. The ship on the left is unidentified. Courtesy Naval Historical Center, photo by Tommy Cobb.

the "Star-Spangled Banner" is played, and the guests and crew stand at attention in a short but moving ceremony. . . .

As the little craft pulls away from the naval base at Anacostia, all legislators seem to relax. One congressman said to me, pointing to the receding shoreline, "The minute I am on the river, I forget I have any connection with the everyday life." . . .

The *Sequoia* has worked so long and well for the United States government that I feel that she too, when she is retired, should receive a medal from the Navy, a pension, and maybe a commemorative stamp.

The Nixon Years and His Final Days Aboard *Sequoia,* 1969–74

After President Johnson left office in January 1969, the Nixon White House staff maintained the same attitude about *Sequoia,* considering the yacht to be exclusively "the president's yacht," even though it was still "owned" by the navy and maintained at the Navy Yard.

This was the time in America when the hippies gathered at Woodstock, and the Beatles' music had swept the country. The United States was still fighting an agonizing war in Vietnam, but at the same time, NASA had put a man on the moon.

The lively lady at full speed (about 10 knots).

The mahogany pilothouse on the main deck is finished with high-gloss varnish.

Sequoia's helm, brass binnacle, and twin throttles.

All color photos by Ann Stevens.

The distinctive curved window on each side of the forward end of the main salon.

The anchor windless and the varnished teak foredeck. The union jack is only flown while *Sequoia* is not underway.

View of the main salon on *Sequoia*. The staircase on the left leads to the lower deck. The bar is to the left of the opening to the aft salon. A spinet piano is sometimes placed next to the staircase.

The guest cabin on the port side of the lower deck.

A view of the large presidential suite.

A dinner setting in the main salon for eighteen guests with a harpist ready to serenade them.

Sequoia's enclosed aft deck, now called the aft salon, as furnished by designer Carlton Varney in the 1980s.

Sequoia's upper deck was sometimes carpeted as shown in this photo taken in 1987. The stairs on the left descend to the aft salon. A steep second staircase next to the stack leads to the pantry.

VIP guests aboard in New York Harbor, July 4, 1986: Senators John Chafee, Sam Nunn, and Carl Levin with Mrs. Levin.

Sequoia saluting the Statue of Liberty, July 4, 1986.

From *Sequoia,* an ABC camerman films USS *Iowa* as President Reagan reviews the assembled fleet in New York Harbor, July 4, 1986.

Sequoia passing Mount Vernon homeward bound on the Potomac River.

Early morning on the Intracoastal Waterway as *Sequoia* heads south for Florida.

Except for formal occasions, President Richard Nixon's use of the yacht, like his predecessor's, was often unpredictable and without much prior notice. However, he did use *Sequoia* more frequently than Johnson. The White House staff early on warned cabinet officers not to think about using the president's yacht when the president was in town.

At the Navy Yard, *Sequoia's* crew was kept ready to get underway on twenty minutes' notice. The president would arrive at times for a cruise without guests, accompanied only by his doctor, Secret Service agents, and sometimes his dog "King Timaho," an Irish setter. Nixon particularly enjoyed the ambiance of the river and the seclusion that the yacht provided. Alone or with family, he would typically relax over a glass of scotch whiskey, then have one of his favorite meals such as steak, green beans, and a baked potato with a fine wine. Chateau Margaux was reported to be among his favorites. When microwave ovens became available, *Sequoia* was one of the first naval vessels to be provided with one so the cooks could produce on short notice the baked potatoes that Nixon enjoyed so much.

Sequoia became the site for some of Nixon's most important meetings. In his book *The White House Years,* Nixon's National Security Advisor Henry Kissinger tells of being called to a meeting aboard *Sequoia* on May 2, 1972. After his discouraging talks in Paris with Le Duc Tho, the North Vietnamese negotiator, Kissinger flew back to Andrews Air Force Base just outside Washington where White House Chief of Staff Alexander Haig took him by helicopter to the Washington Navy Yard. The president was waiting aboard *Sequoia.* There at the dining table Kissinger reported on his meetings to Nixon.[6] Walter Isaacson, Kissinger's biographer, states that the three men agreed then and there to cancel an impending Moscow summit and decided "that a major military response [in Vietnam] was necessary."[7] Later it was decided that the response would be the mining of Haiphong Harbor and other major Vietnamese harbors.

On another occasion, after a long day of tense discussions about whether to attack the Vietnam forces operating out of Cambodia, Kissinger recalled relaxing aboard *Sequoia* with Nixon, John Mitchell, and Charles "Bebe" Rebozo during an enjoyable cruise to Mt. Vernon that relieved the tension of the day with a nice change of scenery and "liquid refreshments."[8]

Kissinger sometimes was able to sequester *Sequoia* for informal meetings, such as on April 9, 1970, when he invited Soviet Ambassador Anatoly Dobrynin on board for a dinner to go over the whole range of United States–Soviet relations.[9]

The commanding officer of *Sequoia* in 1973 was Lieutenant Commander Andrew Combe, USN. He claimed he had the best navy job for a lieutenant commander in Washington. Combe was kept very busy by the White House, logging more than one hundred trips in *Sequoia* with Nixon on board and dozens more with cabinet members and the White House senior staff. He believes half the

Presidents Nixon and Brezhnev watch from *Sequoia's* upper deck as the yacht gets underway on June 19, 1973. Courtesy Nixon Presidential Materials Staff of the National Archives.

Congress was aboard at one time or another during his eighteen-month watch.

White House plans for Nixon's historic 1973 meeting in Washington with Soviet President Leonid Brezhnev included a cruise aboard *Sequoia*. "When we learned the Brezhnev cruise was scheduled," one crew member related, "we spent two weeks from sunup to sundown preparing for it. Every bit of brightwork was stripped down, sanded, and revarnished. Even new custom-made bamboo furniture was ordered for the upper deck. However, when it was delivered, Mrs. Nixon sat in it and declared it uncomfortable. Next day it was shipped away and new furniture was brought aboard that passed her test." With two heads of state coming aboard, Combe was concerned over the correct protocol for flying the two national flags. He looked for a reference, but could find no precedent or instructions. So he took it upon himself to fly the American flag from the starboard yardarm and the Soviet flag from the port yardarm. No one complained.

For the crew, June 19, 1973, was a momentous day. As President Leonid Brezhnev stepped aboard accompanied by Foreign Minister Andrei Gromyko, Ambassador Anatoly Dobrynin, and a

Soviet and American fellowship blossomed aboard *Sequoia*. The two heads of state wave to onlookers as *Sequoia* passes under the South Capital Street bridge. Courtesy Nixon Presidential Materials Staff of the National Archives.

translator, the crew saluted and broke out a big red Soviet flag on *Sequoia*'s port yardarm. The Soviets were welcomed by the president, who was already on board with his Secretary of State William Rogers, Secretary of the Treasury William Simon, National Security Advisor Henry Kissinger, and Press Secretary Ron Ziegler. Lieutenant Commander Combe said he particularly felt the weight of his responsibility that day with the two most powerful men in the world on board his vessel. The main topic under consideration during the visit was the limitation of strategic arms, which the two men discussed over dinner as *Sequoia* cruised leisurely along the Potomac River with a press boat and several security vessels in attendance.[10]

Combe described another less-historic event that occurred while Nixon was on board. "News came that Ted Heath had won the election as Prime Minister of Great Britain. That was before communications by satellite. Nixon wanted to be among the first to congratulate Heath so he asked me if it was possible to make the transatlantic phone call from *Sequoia*. I told him we had never tried it, but let's see. At my request, the

White House 'patched' the *Sequoia*'s radio phone through to Downing Street. Much to my surprise it worked just fine, and it was a 'first.'"

Combe was particularly sensitive to Kissinger's complaint that the yacht's engines were at times too noisy for good conversation. The only thing Combe said he could do about that was to run the yacht very slowly, at five or six knots (about seven miles per hour) which would keep the engine noise down to a comfortable rumble. Despite the engine noise, Kissinger says in his book *The White House Years* that he felt *Sequoia* "served a useful purpose in enabling presidents to escape the claustrophobic tension of the White House. For the White House imprisons as well as exults. . . . Periodic release from its tensions is a necessity. *Sequoia* provided a quick sanctuary; it was handier than Camp David, easier for casual, informal discussions. It is a shame it was later dispensed with. It was made to order for the fateful discussions." In that vein, Kissinger also noted that Nixon particularly enjoyed relaxing on *Sequoia*'s "sun deck" with a rum-and-coke in hand before dinner.

To Kissinger, the furniture aboard *Sequoia* seemed squat, heavy, and undistinguished. At that time heavy rattan furniture was in use in the after salon. A thick chocolate-brown carpet covered the floor of the main salon and a small spinet piano was positioned alongside the staircase, said to have been put aboard for President Truman. A picture of George Washington hung in the main salon.

During her many years of government service *Sequoia*'s interior was never known for the elegance that might be expected of the presidential yacht of a superpower. The navy considered her more a service craft for government officials to use for private meetings, informal entertaining, fishing, and cooling off. Thus, she was modestly furnished with little attention to style, despite sometimes being the site for entertaining important foreign guests. It was not until the 1980s, when the Presidential Yacht Trust was responsible for her, that her interior was dressed with expensive furniture and fine accessories to give her more of an aura of high style and dignity.

Jim Krokowski, a crew member in the seventies, said that when *Sequoia* was underway, she was usually accompanied by at least one escort boat. "When the president was on board, we then had two escort boats manned by Coast Guard crews plus a cabin cruiser called *Rockfish,* all of which carried members of the presidential Secret Service detail," he said. The Coast Guard crews had police powers of arrest, which the naval personnel did not have. When the president was on board, four Secret Service agents were usually present aboard *Sequoia.*

Combe said during the Nixon years, the underway crew normally consisted of himself, two quartermasters, an electrician, an engineer, three line handlers, two cooks, and two serving stewards. Four or five other crew members stood by back at the Navy Yard to help tie up *Sequoia* upon her return. Combe used two sets of

Britain's Prince Charles and Princess Anne with members of the crew on *Sequoia*'s foredeck in July 1970. Courtesy Nixon Presidential Materials Staff of the National Archives.

docking lines for the yacht, the ordinary working lines and a set of clean white dress lines for special occasions.

Nixon, who was known to love pomp and circumstance, particularly enjoyed the navy custom of paying respects to the founding father of our country when passing Washington's tomb at Mt. Vernon. When he entertained foreign dignitaries he would often sail them to Mt. Vernon to impress them with the naval rendering-of-honors ceremony. On one such occasion, a crew member related that after the ship's bell had been tolled and the last note of taps sounded, the president turned to the young sailor next to him at the rail who had been saluting and said, "I know they don't pay you very much son, but don't you think this makes it all worthwhile?"

According to crew members, Nixon would come aboard at times without family or friends during the tense days of the Watergate scandal and would pick out tunes on the piano. He often played "God Bless America," but he played it so many times that it grew tiresome for the crew. They noted Nixon seldom came up to the wheelhouse at that time to chat with the crew as he had earlier, but otherwise he was quite friendly and often offered to shake hands.

Members of the president's family sometimes would use *Sequoia* to entertain visiting dignitaries, to host community service programs, or just for their own pleasure. One "dignity trip," as the crew liked to called them, was a cruise with royalty. When Britain's Prince Charles and Princess Anne came to Washington in July 1970, they were invited to *Sequoia* by First Daughters Julie and Tricia Nixon for a luncheon cruise to Mt. Vernon, along with a group of their young friends. The *Washington Star* made much out of the fact that the British flag, flown on *Sequoia*'s yardarm that day as a traditional naval courtesy, was unintentionally flown upside down. That is something only an expert would notice.

In her book *Special People,* Julie Nixon Eisenhower described that cruise as taking place on a hot, muggy summer day, indicating it was not a very gregarious occasion. At one point, she said, the prince was asked how he justified the monarchy—certainly a sticky question for that sticky day.

Prince Charles replied that the monarchy provided stability and an anchor with the past for the British. Then, he added, for some people it fills a "fairy-tale role." At about that point Princess Anne left the group. The next thing her hostesses knew, she had "jumped ship," and was at the helm of one of the escorting Coast Guard boats having great fun trying to get her well-coifed lady-in-waiting wet with spray.

Mrs. Nixon employed *Sequoia* in quite a different way by scheduling cruises for underprivileged youngsters and for disabled service personnel. She regularly invited patients on board from the Bethesda Naval Hospital and the Walter Reed Army Hospital. Crew members said she always made sure refreshments were provided and sometimes she even arranged to have a military combo on board.

"Mrs. Nixon was very nice to us," said John Coco, a crew member at the time. "She would straighten up things the stewards missed. A few times she sailed with just her daughter Tricia." Before Tricia's wedding the Nixons gave a small luncheon for the Cox family on board *Sequoia,* and later another one for the newlyweds only. After most parties any surplus food usually was made available to the crew, so we often enjoyed such treats as seafood creole and beef stroganoff and could eat as well as the president and his guests."

When it was definitely known the Nixons were not going to use the yacht, she was made available to cabinet members. The captain mentioned that Secretary of Defense Melvin Laird was particularly fond of *Sequoia.* "Sometimes he was able to have her for a downriver poker party which might last until two or three in the morning."

"When a group of guests arrived to board *Sequoia,* the ship's officers usually greeted them alongside on the dock rather than on board so as not to overcrowd the gangway and the narrow deck," said Robert King Baer, one of the Coast Guard boatswain's mates who served aboard *Sequoia* in 1970. He also remembered the crew scrubbing the waterline every day and painting it at least six times during the summer. "Before every 'dignity trip'" he said, "we also sanded and painted all the stanchions.

"The Presidential Service Badge became part of the permanent uniform of *Sequoia's* crew and the support staff after we had been on duty for one year, and I wore mine with great pride."

Evidently the navy assigned promising young men to *Sequoia.* One such crew member who was aboard as a second-class electronics technician, related how his commanding officer Andrew Combe "nearly forced" him to apply for officers' training in the navy's Scientific Education Program. He did, and after that, technician Johnny L. Green's career took

Traditional naval honors are rendered for George Washington while passing his tomb at Mt. Vernon. Courtesy Nixon Presidential Materials Staff of the National Archives.

Pat Nixon with her special guests gathered on *Sequoia*'s fish deck. Courtesy the Library of Congress.

Luncheon for the newlyweds aboard *Sequoia*. *Left to right:* Ed Cox, the president, Tricia Nixon Cox, and Mrs. Nixon. Courtesy Nixon Presidential Materials Staff of the National Archives.

off. He first became a naval aviator and later a captain. By 2003 he was in command of the nuclear carrier, USS *Theodore Roosevelt*.

Nixon's Final Days Aboard *Sequoia*

As the Watergate scandal closed in on President Nixon, Combe got strict instructions from the president never to run the yacht where he would have to see the Watergate complex. Nixon's saddest trip was undoubtedly on August 5, 1974, while cruising on the Potomac River, when he told his family and his secretary Rose Mary Woods that he had decided to resign the presidency.

Bebe Rebozo had flown up from Miami to Washington on August 1, 1974, to be with his good friend the president. At seven that evening the two men boarded *Sequoia*. As they cruised along the Potomac River, Nixon told Rebozo he was planning to resign. At first Rebozo urged him to resist, but later he became convinced there was no alternative.

"I remember Bebe Rebozo and the president took an evening cruise together on the first of August," said Lieutenant Dewey Beliech, *Sequoia*'s second-in-command. "Probably during that cruise was when the president made his final decision to resign. The night before, the president came aboard by himself and sat in the after salon staring out as if in deep thought. Everyone in the crew seemed to know what was coming," he said.

"The next night, August 5," Beliech said, "the president with his family and his secretary, Rose Mary Woods, came on board for a dinner cruise to Mt. Vernon. Perhaps that was a way to spare them from the evening newscasts. During the trip the president played the piano and everyone sang 'God Bless America' and otherwise tried to have a good time." That cruise was probably the most emotional time in all of *Sequoia*'s history. Daughter Julie Nixon Eisenhower wrote in her book *Special People*, "We were subject to a death watch. . . . Being on the *Sequoia* was like bobbing along in a glass bottle," with reporters and photographers following along in boats.

On August 8, the president stepped down. The Nixons' departure from Washington included one last look at *Sequoia*. "By coincidence," Beliech recalls, "the day the Nixons left the White House was also the day scheduled for the naval change-of-command ceremony aboard *Sequoia* at the Navy Yard. [Beliech was to take command.] All crew members were on deck waiting for the ceremony to begin when to everyone's surprise, the presidential helicopter buzzed low overhead on its way to Andrews Air Force Base. The Nixons waved a last farewell to the crew and to the little ship the president knew so well and loved so much," Beliech said.

The Ford Years, 1974–77

When the Ford administration took over the White House in the summer of 1974, one of its goals was to put the Nixon scandal to rest. The economy was then in a recession. As spring arrived, the last Americans were being evacuated from Vietnam. Only then did the president's men get around to taking stock of the presidential yacht to decide if she was worth keeping in service.

Staff memos were drawn up describing the yacht, her capabilities, and how she might be employed. A memo with *Sequoia*'s history attached, written for Chief of Staff Donald Rumsfeld, pointed out the yacht would be only a ten-minute drive from the White House and that *Sequoia*'s normal season ran from April 1 to October 31. Another White House memo noted *Sequoia* was restricted to inland waterways, could carry up to forty people, had a maximum speed of eleven knots, and burned six gallons of diesel fuel per hour when cruising at five knots. That memo ended with the recommendation that *Sequoia* not be sold, but retained, stating the following:

> [She is] a beautiful and gracious way to entertain, to discuss government affairs, to influence groups to support Administration domestic and foreign policy; even if the President doesn't use the boat often, it can be used effectively to his advantage by the Cabinet, the Congressional Office, the staff, etc. [She] provides a good way for the President to relax; a potentially great asset in place and not the subject of any criticism or debate.

A decision was thus made to retain the yacht with control continuing to rest with the White House, not the navy. She would be scheduled by the president's military assistant.

President Ford took his first presidential cruise aboard *Sequoia* on May 7, 1975, some ten months after Nixon had said his good-byes in August of the preceding year. Ford wanted his first cruise to be an informal get-together of his cabinet and the White House senior staff, including wives. He described the event as "a time for the team to relax and get to know each other better." Members of the press were not invited, but daughter Susan Ford was encouraged to bring along her camera to practice her photography. David Hume Kennerly, a White House photographer, was there to take the official photos for the record. Ford was the first and only president to have his entire cabinet on board *Sequoia* at one time. It made the Secret Service a bit nervous; however, there were no problems. The weather was fine, and the president's guests enjoyed the cruise and the chance to huddle together in the new and informal setting.

A few days later, Richard Cheney wrote in a staff memorandum: "We definitely want to keep the boat in service this year and we would like to use it from time to time for working dinners and with dignitaries from the U.S. or abroad. . . . The Cabinet should definitely be able to use it. That should include those senior White House staff members who are members of the Cabinet. . . . If someone [else] wants to use it, they'll have to submit for approval each time . . . to me for sign off. . . ."

Soon after, in June 1975, Susan Ford decided *Sequoia* was a good place to have a small party. As reported by the *Washington Post* in its Style section, Susan with her date and three Holton Arms classmates with their dates dined on beef stroganoff while cruising to Mt. Vernon in celebration of Susan's graduation from Holton Arms. The following month the *Post* reported that Susan Ford had a disco party on board *Sequoia* and watched the Fourth of July fireworks with her friends from the upper deck.

In 1975, the Ford White House staff began to have problems over the use of

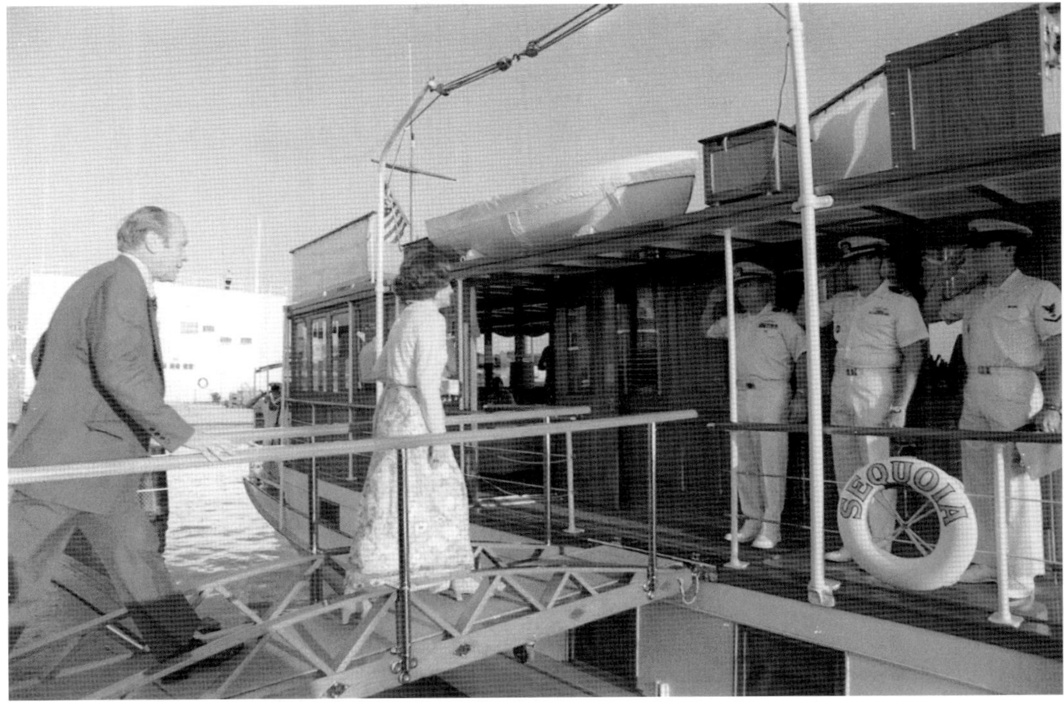

President and Betty Ford boarding *Sequoia* on May 7, 1975, to cruise with the cabinet and White House Staff. Courtesy Gerald R. Ford Library.

Sequoia. A memo sent to the new Chief of Staff Dick Cheney spelled out that the Ford children had taken a liking to the yacht and at times "on very, very short notice" would ask to use *Sequoia*. Sometimes these requests caused scheduling conflicts.

Cabinet members, senior White House staff, and Congressional leaders had the president's approval to use *Sequoia*, but the question was: Can First Family members preempt the yacht at the last minute, or should Steve, Jack, and Susan be advised that the boat would not always be available to them? The memo suggested Cheney get the president's policy on the matter. There is no record of the president's decision, but in practice it appears the "First Kids" were told to put in their requests for the yacht well in advance and wait their turn.

White House staff members made estimates of what it cost to entertain on *Sequoia* assuming the food was provided by the White House mess. In 1975, their analysis showed a sit-down dinner for twenty-two persons cost approximately $330 including cocktails and hors d'oeuvres prior to dinner, the dinner with wine, and liqueur or champagne afterwards. It was noted that twenty persons would fit around the table better than twenty-two.

President Ford confers with, *from left,* Economics Affairs Assistant L. William Seidman, National Security Assistant Brent Scowcroft, Administrator of the Federal Energy Administration Frank G. Zarb, and Chairman of the Council of Economic Advisors Alan Greenspan aboard *Sequoia* on May 7, 1975. Courtesy Gerald R. Ford Library.

Standing behind President Ford and William Seidman on *Sequoia's* upper deck, Chief of Staff Donald Rumsfeld chats with National Security Advisor Richard Allen. Courtesy Gerald R. Ford Library.

For an onboard buffet dinner for forty persons, including cocktails and hors d'oeuvres, two entrees, vegetables, salad, wine with dinner, and dessert, the cost would be approximately $400.

Cocktails for forty persons with expensive hors d'oeuvres such as giant shrimp or shish kebabs would cost approximately $320. The staff also did a cost-comparison of entertaining twenty-two persons at Blair House with entertaining them aboard *Sequoia.* They found the cost would be about twice as high at Blair House.

President Ford did use the yacht to promote political goodwill. In July 1975, he was host to a bipartisan group of congressional leaders with their wives. His guests included Senate Majority Leader Mike Mansfield, President Pro Tempore of the Senate James Eastland, and Speaker of the House Carl Albert. Others

Emperor Hirohito and his wife on an afternoon cruise aboard *Sequoia* during their Washington visit in October 1975. The Japanese caption for this photo stated: "Riding down the beautiful Potomac River with its verdant banks on the exclusive Presidential Yacht *Sequoia,* the golden chrysanthemum imperial banner fluttering in the breeze under clear skies above both countries' flags, the Imperial Highnesses enjoyed themselves coming out on deck two or three times." The Mainichi Newspapers.

in Ford's administration also used *Sequoia* for diplomatic purposes. For instance, in June 1997, she was used by the State Department to host a dinner for a delegation from the USSR, headed by Deputy Prime Minister Ignaty Novikov, the third highest ranking official in the Soviet Union. The host was Arthur Hartman of the State Department, who recently had been the U.S. Ambassador to the Soviet Union. During that first full year of the Ford presidency, the White House used *Sequoia* for nineteen cruises.

When Emperor Hirohito and the Empress of Japan came to Washington for a state visit in early October 1975, among the arrangements made for the royal couple was a cruise aboard *Sequoia* downriver to the mansion at Mt. Vernon. Lonnie Cooper, a crew member, said,

"We were told not to look directly at 'their majesties' while we were in their presence." He also recalled that a crew member of Japanese descent was very keen to be on board for this cruise, but the Japanese security officers said they did not want any Asian people on or near the yacht for the occasion. They also were concerned whether any of the gun-carrying American agents aboard were former war veterans who might hold a grudge against the Japanese. *Sequoia*'s crew members were briefed on security arrangements that included looking at pictures of several men considered potential Hirohito assassins.

President Ford did not go on that trip; instead, the host was the State Department's Chief of Protocol Henry Catto assisted by his deputy William Codus. The yacht sailed under three flags that afternoon—the emperor's red banner with its golden chrysanthemum was at the truck (the top of the mast), the Japanese national flag on the port yardarm, and the Stars and Stripes on the starboard yardarm.

Lieutenant Commander Dewey Beliech, *Sequoia*'s officer-in-charge at the time, recalls that "none of us knew exactly what to expect when the emperor and the empress were embarked, but it turned out the emperor was very informal and easy. He even turned and introduced himself to me after I saluted him at the gangway."

When Canadian Prime Minister Pierre Trudeau came to Washington in 1976, the president invited him for a small working dinner-cruise aboard *Sequoia* on Wednesday, June 16. The White House staff drew up the plans for the evening. The chief steward aboard *Sequoia* was required to submit several menus to the White House for their consideration and coordination with the Canadian staff. It was important to ensure the food would be agreeable to the guests. Meanwhile, the crew concentrated on polishing brass, scrubbing the awnings and the canvas skirts around the railing, and touching up the paint to eliminate the slightest blemish so the president could be proud of his yacht. Four stewards were put to work on the interior, fastidiously cleaning and arranging furniture for maximum comfort.

By noon on that Wednesday, the table was set with eight places for dinner, using the best White House linen and china. The captain also had checked the bar to be sure it was fully stocked with top-of-the-line brands including Canadian whiskey. He had ordered all hands to be in white service uniforms and ready for his inspection one hour before the president was scheduled to arrive. That afternoon Secret Service agents came on board to make a full security check, including the results of the underwater examination of the hull done on a daily basis by a navy diver. Then they reviewed with the Coast Guard detachment the underway escort requirements and emergency evacuation plans. Earlier that morning the captain had received his copy of the White House schedule timed down to the minute:

President Ford and Prime Minister Trudeau having a predinner chat on *Sequoia*'s top deck. The foursome in the background are Secretary of State Henry Kissinger, *left front,* talking with American Ambassador to Canada Thomas O. Enders, *on Kissinger's left,* and Ivan Head, special assistant to Pierre Elliott Trudeau, prime minister of Canada, *on Kissinger's right.* Courtesy Gerald R. Ford Library.

THE PRESIDENT'S DINNER FOR PRIME MINISTER TRUDEAU ABOARD SEQUOIA

6:30 pm	The President and Prime Minister board motorcade and depart South Grounds en route Washington Navy Yard.
6:40 pm	Motorcade arrives Pier One.
	OPEN PRESS COVERAGE
	CLOSED ARRIVAL
	The President and Prime Minister Trudeau will be met by Lieut. Cmdr. Skip Beliech, Commanding Officer, *SEQUOIA*
	NOTE: The President and the Prime Minister will board first and pause for a 30-second photo opportunity. Other guests will then proceed aboard.
6:43 pm	*SEQUOIA* DEPARTS Pier One en route to the Wilson Bridge area.
7:15 pm	Dinner is served.
9:15 pm	*SEQUOIA* ARRIVES Pier One.
	PRESS POOL COVERAGE
	CLOSED ARRIVAL
9:18 pm	The President escorts Prime Minister Trudeau to his motorcade, bids farewell.

[Author's Note: This schedule, allowing only three minutes for *Sequoia* to be tied up and the gangway rigged for departures, seems unrealistic.]

In addition to the president and the prime minister, the dinner guests included the Canadian ambassador, the Canadian minister of finance, the special assistant to the prime minister, the U.S. secretary of state, the U.S. national security advisor, and the American ambassador to Canada. Dinner and wines served that evening were as follows:

Broiled Danish lobster tails	Johannesburg Riesling 1972
Crown roast of lamb	Beaulieu Vineyard
Parisienne potatoes	Pinot Noir 1973
Fresh snow peas	Robert Mondavi
Port Salut cheese	
Hearts of palm	
Cherry tomatoes	
Baked Alaska with cherries jubilee	Schramsberg Blanc de Blanc 1973

Trudeau said later that his Washington visit resulted in one of the greatest advances in Canadian foreign relations because, at the time, President Ford invited him to participate in the economic summit which was about to be held in Puerto Rico. That led to Canada's admission into the powerful group of seven leading industrialized nations.[11]

President and Mrs. Ford also used *Sequoia* in June 1976 for a surprise "Big Five-O" birthday party for the vice president's wife, "Happy" Rockefeller. Actress Kitty Carlisle was among the sixteen guests invited for an elegant dinner party and cruise on the Potomac River.

In preparation for such special occasions, Boatswain's Mate Ken Ruse, then a crew member, said that "for the visits of Trudeau and Hirohito he oversaw that every bit of brightwork on *Sequoia* was stripped, sanded, and revarnished. All the stanchions were freshly repainted for these 'dignity' trips." Barry Nierengarten, also a crew member, noted that for the

Trudeau dinner, the table was set with the "Franciscan Masterpiece" china, which he described as cream colored with a thin silver rim and a silver presidential seal. He said that china was often in use on board during the Ford presidency.

Boatswain's Mate John Coco commented that "Once when one of President Ford's sons was cruising with friends, he gave the captain a hard time because he didn't want the party to end at midnight as was scheduled. The captain called the naval aide at the White House for advice and got specific White House orders to return the yacht to the dock as previously scheduled." No exceptions were to be made, even for the president's son.

White House records indicate that in September 1976, forty guests were invited aboard *Sequoia* to watch the televised debate between Democratic candidate Jimmy Carter and President Ford. The guest list included ambassadors, senators, generals, as well as two well-known Washingtonians who later married each other: the *Washington Post*'s editor Ben Bradlee and writer Sally Quinn. However, Ben Bradlee does not recall that he actually attended.

As the Ford administration began to pack up in late 1976 and Jimmy Carter prepared to move into the White House, there was much speculation down at the Navy Yard that the new president, a Naval Academy graduate, would put *Sequoia* to good and frequent use. After working late shifts in March 1977 to ready the yacht for Carter's use in April, crew members first learned from headlines in the *Evening Star* on April 1 that Carter had ordered *Sequoia* to be sold at auction. At first they wondered if this was an April Fools' joke.

Crew member Lonnie Cooper said that Hugh Carter, the president's nephew, had recently inspected the yacht and said "Uncle Jimmy is going to love this." Cooper also thought the news report was an April Fools' joke, but after his skipper went to the White House and returned with a copy of the order, he knew it was not so, and it would effectively put the Administrative Unit and *Sequoia* out of business. He said, "We sat down and

THE WHITE HOUSE
WASHINGTON
March 30, 1977

MEMORANDUM FOR
THE SECRETARY OF DEFENSE

SUBJECT: Presidential Yacht

Please deactivate the SEQUOIA and have it disposed of through public sale. Despite its distinguished career, I feel that Presidential yacht SEQUOIA is no longer needed.

Jimmy Carter

President Carter's memo to Harold Brown sealing *Sequoia*'s fate.

figured out when *Sequoia's* final cruise as the presidential yacht [took place]. It was last November" [1976]. With the crew's morale sinking, over the next few months their final job was to keep the yacht clean and to show her to prospective bidders.

Years later, during his retirement, Gerald Ford was asked how he viewed *Sequoia*. "[She] was a superb yacht for special entertaining of presidential White House guests. The *Sequoia* was more informal than the White House itself, but significant as a recognition of the prestige of the special guest. . . . I strongly believe *[Sequoia]* was a White House asset that could be used for constructive presidential entertainment."[12]

CHAPTER SIX

Sequoia in the Private Sector, 1977–81

The Sequoia *is the most patriotic and symbolic piece of government property ever to be privately owned.*
—President Jimmy Carter, 1977[1]

Well before *Sequoia's* crew was shocked by President Carter's order to sell the yacht early in 1977, Lieutenant Commander Beliech and his sailors had ordered a special *Sequoia* jacket for Amy Carter with her name embroidered on it. They planned to present it to her when she first came on board.

But the new president and his daughter never came aboard. Perhaps it was because Carter didn't want to be associated with the yacht that Nixon had liked so much. Perhaps he considered it unnecessary after hearing it cost about $800,000 annually to operate. Perhaps he thought his use of the yacht would send the wrong message about his presidency. As the *Navy Times* commented in the May 1977 issue, "*Sequoia* became another victim of Carter's money-saving measures, along with excess limousines and heating of the White House. . . . Although most people feel little remorse at seeing *Sequoia* sold, her Navy crew of approximately thirty men do. . . . They feel as though they are almost a part of her. . . ."

Whatever the real reasons, the official explanation stated: "The *Sequoia* can only be used on inland waterways. In this regard, the United States Coast Guard declared the vessel unseaworthy in 1968. Moreover, in view of its limited potential uses, the Navy crew required to keep the *Sequoia* in its current condition appears to be extremely expensive."[2]

Exploitation, Decay, and Return, 1977–81

The Defense Logistics Agency (DLA) was appointed the action agency. The DLA requested sealed bids for the purchase of the boat by May 18, 1977, and issued this statement:

> Prior to sale, the *Sequoia* . . . will lose all evidence of its former high estate. For example, the china, the flatware and the glasses bearing the White House seal are removed. The piano (once Harry Truman's) in the main salon and some other furniture, including a color TV, have been removed. The ship's bell, some lamps, and the bench lockers from the forecastle will go to the Navy Museum. These actions should prevent the vessel from becoming a mere souvenir or being used in a manner inconsistent with Presidential property.

It is curious that government officials were concerned over possible misuse of *Sequoia's* bench lockers, ship's bell, and lamps. How would they be misused? It is more likely they wanted some memorabilia of this unique naval vessel represented in the Navy Museum for display. Despite the many protests over selling *Sequoia* that came in the form of letters to the White House and the Congress, no instructions to the DLA were issued from the White House to cancel the sale.

Detail from the special jacket *Sequoia's* crew ordered for Amy Carter.

Before the bidding started, experts placed the value of *Sequoia* at between $200,000 and $400,000. Of the 174 bids submitted, Thomas A. Malloy, a forty-nine-year-old condominium developer in Providence, Rhode Island, and his six partners were the winners with a bid of $286,000. The losing bidders included oil executive Dr. Armand Hammer, who bid $251,000, and *Hustler* magazine publisher Larry Flint, who bid $200,000. Another bidder, Norman F. Pulliam, also had offered $200,000 for *Sequoia,* and he would later become her owner. Pulliam claimed he would have bid more earlier had the navy not stripped the yacht of most of her furnishings, as he had hoped to make her into a floating museum.

The winning bid for *Sequoia* was announced in May 1977 at the Portsmouth, Rhode Island, naval base. The July issue of *Defense Logistics Agency News* reported the scene: "An *Associated Press* representative hurried to the bid board to identify the winning bidder. . . . Camera crews from three TV stations filmed the scene as the contracting officer called out the winning bid, number 171." *Sea Service* magazine somewhat ironically reported the sale of *Sequoia* on its obituary page.

However, there was a "hiccup" to the sale when Undersecretary of the Interior James Joseph requested that the sale be held up to determine if *Sequoia* qualified as a historic monument. He alleged that the government had failed to follow all the proper legal procedures for selling federal property of potential historical value. John Chafee, Nixon's former secretary of the navy and by then a U.S. senator from Rhode Island, became involved in the matter. After his discussions with the navy and the Justice Department, the Department of Interior approved the sale with the provision that the buyer "agrees to make no substantive changes to the yacht without navy approval." Chafee was then able to announce "Everything is squared away. Malloy cannot make any changes in the profile of the boat, nor can he change the varnish or color of the yacht unless he first gets permission from the navy."[3] Thus Malloy signed a pre-award agreement that no major alterations would be made without navy approval. With that caveat, the protests subsided. Over time as new owners came and went the caveat was forgotten, but to date no major changes have been made to her 1977 look.

On the morning of July 6, 1977, after the items not to be conveyed into private hands were removed, a four-man navy crew, with the new owner's son onboard as a passenger, set off from Washington to deliver *Sequoia* to her new owners in Providence, Rhode Island.

However, the early controversy over selling *Sequoia* had an echo. Three years after the sale, columnist Colin Campbell wrote in the *New York Times:* "Jimmy Carter has faced mighty troubles in Washington. It was said from the start that part of the problem was his poor grasp of Congress." Campbell then quoted Henry Hall Wilson, a colorful character who had managed congressional relations for Presidents Kennedy and Johnson, as remarking that Carter's sale of *Sequoia* was his first misstep. Campbell further quoted Wilson:

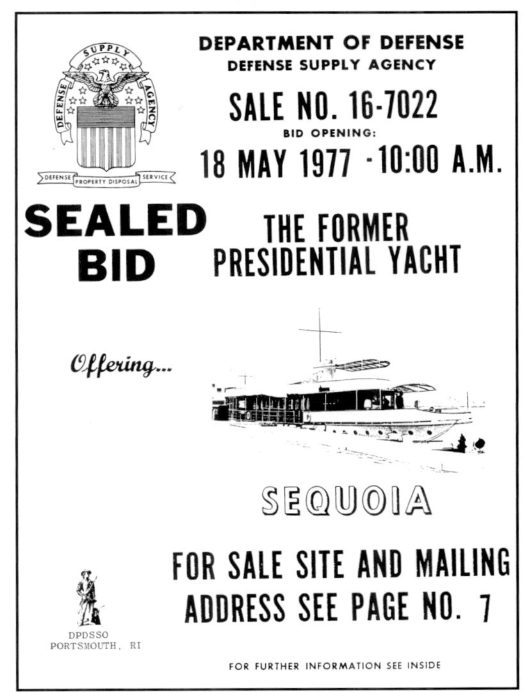

DEPARTMENT OF DEFENSE
DEFENSE SUPPLY AGENCY
SALE NO. 16-7022
BID OPENING:
18 MAY 1977 - 10:00 A.M.

SEALED BID

THE FORMER PRESIDENTIAL YACHT

Offering...

SEQUOIA

FOR SALE SITE AND MAILING ADDRESS SEE PAGE NO. 7

DPDSSO
PORTSMOUTH, RI

FOR FURTHER INFORMATION SEE INSIDE

Department of Defense bid cover.

> The country can be run by almost any President, but only with a yacht. Why? Because the surest, cheapest way for a President to make friends and soften enemies in Congress was out on the water in the *Sequoia,* where legislators could have their drinks in small groups, watch the sky turn red over the Potomac, note with wonder that "*Sequoia*" contained all five vowels and be made to feel like potentates. It was absolute magic.

Malloy, a colorful Rhode Islander, said he was surprised that he won the auction, but was pleased that he was now free to invite his friends to sip cocktails and take floating history lessons aboard a yacht which they have been paying for with tax dollars since 1931.

Malloy did not hesitate to charge the public for visits to *Sequoia* while she lay in Providence harbor and later at Newport. "This is a profit-making venture," he declared, "I'm an opportunist. I saw the ad for the yacht's auction and I said, 'Hell, this could be a real winner.' The president's yacht has never been stepped on by the people of this country. We'll make it worthwhile with some history and memorabilia of the presidents who used it. There's so much history in there it's unbelievable."[4] Malloy said he spent $50,000 to make *Sequoia* into a museum. He charged $2.00 a person for a twenty-minute tour of the yacht which included a taped narration, but the public response disappointed him.

Early in 1978, Malloy sold *Sequoia* for $355,000 to Norman F. Pulliam of South Carolina, one of the unsuccessful bidders in 1977. Pulliam was more interested in exploiting the history of *Sequoia* than using her as his private yacht. He called her "the Floating White House" and moored her at a specially built site at North Myrtle Beach, South Carolina. Retired Navy Captain James Chapman was asked to take charge. Fittingly enough, Chapman was one of Jimmy Carter's classmates at the U.S. Naval Academy.

That May an effort was launched by Representative Philip Burton, a democrat from California, to have Congress buy back *Sequoia* for $1 million and have it operated by the U.S. Park Service, but the plan was killed by the House Interior Committee. Representative Mickey Edwards, a Republican committee member from Oklahoma, was quoted as saying "I, too, care about historical preservation, but are we going to track down and buy at taxpayers' expense every stroller in which a president was pushed as a child, every car in which a president rode, and every bed in which a president slept?"[5]

Meanwhile, U.S. Senator Strom Thurmond of South Carolina helped Pulliam get back some, but not all, of the furniture the government had removed from the yacht before the auction. The senator was an enthusiastic supporter of having the yacht in his state and gladly participated in the dedication of the new dockside museum at Myrtle Beach. A feature of the exhibit was a short film highlighting national political events during *Sequoia's* forty-six years of government service. The boarding charge was now up to $2.50 per person.

Attendance was good the first year; it even reached 1,100 visitors on one day. But the museum was not open in the winter, and once the regular summer visitors had seen the yacht, they didn't return, Chapman said. "The Presidential Yacht Museum," as it was then called, was opened for two seasons, and during that time it was visited by some 200,000 people, but it wasn't enough. *Sequoia* was again put up for sale.

In March 1980, Chapman was commissioned to take the grand old yacht farther south to La Coquille Club near Palm Beach, Florida, where she was to be put up for auction. The local press described her at the time as "splendidly equipped and in perfect running condition." *Sequoia* was offered for sale by Sotheby Parke Bernet auctioneers along with a consignment of impressionist and modern paintings and some very fine jewelry. The auctioneers expected the yacht to sell for $1 million.

The press release announcing the auction contained a quantity of hype about *Sequoia,* claiming that the British royal family had been aboard as guests of President Johnson and that President Roosevelt and Churchill had met on board, neither of which were true. Nor was it likely, as claimed, that the piano on board was actually the one on which President Truman had played the "Missouri Waltz," but these myths persisted for years.

The top bid for *Sequoia* of $700,000 was refused by owner Norman Pulliam who, in a private deal, reportedly succeeded in getting $750,000 for her from the Ocean Learning Institute of Palm Beach. John Grant, a 1956 Naval Academy graduate, was the institute's president at the time. He proudly declared the yacht would be used to raise money for his nonprofit scientific and technical institute. He said he would build a $3 million working marine museum around *Sequoia* at Palm Beach. He expected to entertain potential donors on board who would help him pay off the bank loan he had obtained to buy *Sequoia.* Among the distinguished members of his institute was U.S. Senator George Murphy. Later, Captain Chapman said it was his impression that the institute was more a social club than a serious scientific organization.

Unfortunately for the new owners, the Palm Beach County Commissioners in November 1980 turned down Grant's proposed museum project for Palm Beach, so Grant was left to find a home elsewhere for *Sequoia.* He found a temporary one at a West Palm Beach bar. The move to that bar marked the lowest ebb in *Sequoia*'s career. She was moored in close company with a sportfisherman named *The Hooker* and another called *Bum Bum.* Grant eventually found a somewhat more respectable place for her at Stuart, Florida, alongside the Lord Chumley Pub. The pub owners hoped *Sequoia*'s presence would attract more customers. The charge to go aboard the yacht was then up to $3.00.

Although the Ocean Learning Institute claimed to have spent $180,000 in a year to maintain *Sequoia,* it wasn't nearly enough. She was losing her glamour, becoming something like a faded movie star. The institute defaulted on their purchase loan in 1981, and there were no further funds available to maintain the yacht.

At that time, having learned of *Sequoia*'s plight, a small group of businessmen came to her rescue with plans to return her to Washington and rejuvenate her. In March 1981, they asked Captain Chapman to check her condition and do whatever was necessary to make her ready for the trip north. Businessman Richard Arendsee, chairman of Four Winds Enterprises, a transportation company, advanced $1.1 million to purchase the yacht. "I'm a patriot and a flag waver," he said. "I started from nothing, and I believe in the free enterprise system. Now I'm giving something back."

With Edward Skinner, an executive of the American Enterprise Institute, Arendsee formed the Presidential Yacht Trust, (a nonprofit 501 (c) (3) organization registered in Washington, D.C.), to preserve and operate *Sequoia*. Other founding members of the trust included Michael Gill, a relative of President Eisenhower; John B. Connally, a former Texas Governor; Robert K. Gray, a former Eisenhower cabinet member; William J. Middendorf II, a former secretary of the navy; Raymond Shafer, a former governor of Pennsylvania; and Jarvis Moody, head of a Washington bank. Their plan was to repay Arendsee eventually through a fund-raising drive to be called "Save the *Sequoia*."

Captain Chapman set off in May 1981 from Florida with Arendsee and his family and several volunteers aboard as crew. As they made their way up the Intracoastal Waterway, problems developed, not so much with the yacht as with some of the volunteers who partied too much and had to be banished in Savannah, Georgia.[6]

Sequoia's arrival back at the capital in June 1981 was cause for celebration, but her new owners were at first disappointed to learn that the privately owned *Sequoia* could not be berthed at the Washington Navy Yard. However, with help from some of the congressional leadership, the secretary of interior was persuaded to provide a berth for her at his government dock located on the west side of the Washington Channel off Hains Point. That actually proved to be a better home for the yacht than at the Navy Yard, as that dock was closer to the White House, more visible to the public, easier to access, and yet secure.

CHAPTER SEVEN

Presidential Yacht Trust, 1981–88

> *The* Sequoia *is a national landmark, and it will be preserved as such. We view it as America's yacht. Once the* Sequoia *is restored, it will be maintained in Washington for official government use.*
>
> —R. Josh Lanier
> Executive Director, Presidential Yacht Trust, 1983

A full circle seemingly had then been made, with *Sequoia* back at her home port with a new lease on life. The dock on Hains Point was *Sequoia*'s home for the next seven years.

Sequoia in Washington, 1981

On August 1, 1981, the Presidential Yacht Trust was ready to host its first evening cruise on the Potomac River. Seventeen senators, their wives, and some White House staff members were invited. It was a splendid occasion. Although President Reagan declined his invitation, he phoned from Camp David to *Sequoia* while she was underway to give his best wishes to the party. Afterwards, Senator Strom Thurmond thanked the trust for "the evening of patriotism, pride, and pleasure" and commended the trustees "for the important role you are playing to preserve this national treasure for future presidents and future generations."[1]

Later that first summer the trust sent the yacht to the York River in Virginia to participate in Yorktown's bicentennial celebration with the hope that President Reagan would visit her while there. Many of the state governors attending that meeting were eager to inspect the famous presidential yacht, but not so President Reagan. He merely pulled up alongside in his limousine, opened the window, and gave her a salute. Unfortunately that was the closest he got to her, then or later. Even back in her home port of Washington, D.C., he never showed enough presidential interest in the yacht to encourage the large donations necessary for the ultimate success of the trust's mission.

Sequoia sailed to New York the following summer to participate in a commemorative party at the Roosevelt home

Charles "Chuck" Vance and Stephen F. Thomas
request the honour of your presence at
Susan Ford Vance's Suprize 25th B-Day
Aboard the Presidential Yacht
"U.S.S. Sequoia"
Saturday the third of July
nineteen hundred and eighty-two
at four o'clock
Music by
"Joe Rinaldi's Famous 'Dixieland Band"
-buffet dinner will be served-

R.s.v.p.- upon receipt of invitation, by phone M V M, Inc., 703-573-0280

The Sequoia will depart at four o'clock - see enclosed card for more details.

Black Tie

One of many efforts by the Presidential Yacht Trust to bring attention to *Sequoia*.

in Hyde Park presided over by Franklin D. Roosevelt, Jr. En route, interior designer Carleton Varney, who had recently redecorated the White House, took on with alacrity the refurbishing of *Sequoia*. Practically overnight during a stop at New York City, he put aboard a dozen Chippendale-style chairs and a ten-piece set of antique wicker furniture. He also brought aboard new lamp shades, glassware, carpets, damask wall coverings, and even bedspreads bearing the presidential seal. He made the interior look elegant for the first time. The *New York Times* quoted Varney as estimating the value of his refurbishing at about $150,000.

When Jody Powell, Jimmy Carter's press secretary, visited the yacht in 1982, he was so favorably impressed with her new interior that he phoned his former boss from the yacht. According to the December 1982 issue of the *Washingtonian* magazine, Powell jokingly told Carter that by selling off the *Sequoia* he had really missed the boat.

The trust soon took up the serious business of fund-raising by soliciting both donations and charters from the public in order to repay Arendsee the $1.1 million he had advanced to buy the yacht and also to pay for current operations and the overhead. *Sequoia* was made available to corporations and individuals who contributed $25,000. The trust also made great efforts to keep the yacht in the limelight. For instance, in 1982 they invited Susan Ford Vance's family to celebrate her twenty-fifth birthday on board with a black-tie gala.

Later Bob Hope's eightieth birthday was celebrated with a party on board, and he was made an "honorary admiral." Attending the party for Hope were such luminaries as General William Westmoreland, actress Phyllis Diller, former Governor Raymond Shafer of Pennsylvania, and J. Peter Grace, chairman of W. R. Grace and Co.

The ex-naval yacht *Honey Fitz* (aka *Barbara Anne* and *Patricia*), which had been sold off in 1970, was also back in Washington, at that time renamed *The Presidents*. She was in commercial charter service and docked on the Washington Channel, a little too close to *Sequoia* for comfort because she gave *Sequoia* competition for attention and funds. Despite the considerable hype over old *Honey Fitz*, she did not have nearly the illustrious pedigree of *Sequoia*. However, *Sequoia* could not be officially offered for public charter because unlike *The Presidents*, she did not have a Coast Guard certificate to carry paying passengers.

The trust was reorganized in mid-1983 to correct its management problems and to have a more politically balanced board. Businessman John Norris Maguire, chairman of the Board of Software AG Systems, became chairman of the trust. Richard Arendsee stayed on, as vice chairman, as did original trust member and businessman Travis Stewart. The new members included Frank Fahrenkopf, chairman of the Republican National Committee, and Charles Manatt, chairman of the Democratic National Committee. Also new to the board were yachtsman Dennis Conner, interior decorator Carleton Varney to serve as curator of the yacht, and lawyer Ben Cotten to serve as general counsel. The new board envisioned *Sequoia* as a site for forums and receptions in Washington and planned to make her available to Reagan and to future presidents. The trust continued to entertain donors on board who contributed $25,000 or more annually toward the costs of her purchase and maintenance.

By the summer of 1983, the trust decided their practice of hiring part-time skippers for Potomac River cruises did not project the smartness and proper maintenance that the yacht should have. They sought a permanent skipper and invited the author, a retired diplomat and retired naval reserve captain, to take command of the yacht. Five crew members were hired to help run the yacht "navy-style," so guests would feel they were aboard a naval vessel fit for presidential use.

During Bob Hope's eightieth birthday celebration aboard *Sequoia*, he was made an honorary admiral. Chairman of the Trust Richard Arendsee is on the left. Courtesy Robert L. Knudsen.

The first order of business for the new crew in spring of 1983 was to bring *Sequoia* back to Washington from New York, where she had been a participant in the celebration of the one hundredth anniversary of the Brooklyn Bridge. *Sequoia* had been asked to attend as a featured guest. The yacht had a special connection because Emily Roebling Cadwalader, the wife of *Sequoia*'s original owner, was the granddaughter of the designer of the Brooklyn Bridge.

A dangerous day at sea for *Sequoia* occurred during that return trip to Washington. *Sequoia* departed from Sandy Hook, New Jersey, on a calm, clear morning and headed south along the New Jersey coast under the command of her new captain. However, as she sailed farther south, she began to roll in the waves coming from the east. In order to reduce the ever-increasing motion, the captain initiated a zigzag course, first running out to sea three miles to put the waves on the port bow, then turning inshore to put the waves on the port quarter. That helped steady the yacht for a time, but the seas continued to build and during one turn she took such a heavy roll that the galley refrigerator door burst open and spewed its contents across the deck. On the next roll the piano broke its constraints and slid across the main salon. To make matters worse the light shield over the large radar in the pilothouse came loose and flew out the door and over the side.

The captain realized he could not continue to put *Sequoia* at risk of capsizing. No one aboard knew the precise limits of her stability, but everyone knew she was top heavy and her low stateroom windows were not watertight. Although it was not yet an emergency, the captain called the Coast Guard to report that *Sequoia* needed a "port of refuge." He reported she was being rolled too much to continue on her southerly course. He asked if it was practical to enter Manasquan Inlet which, from the yacht's position, was the nearest shelter. The Coast Guard station there replied that the entrance had dangerous seas running, and in any case the harbor was too small for a yacht of more than one hundred feet. At that point a listener broke in, calling from the sportfisherman *Heaven Sent* lying just inside the harbor. The listener said he thought there was enough room for the yacht there and said he would stand by inside the entrance to assist as needed.

As there wasn't much choice, *Sequoia* was put on a course to Manasquan Inlet with seas building at her stern. When she reached the inlet, waves were breaking against the two parallel stone breakwaters that framed the narrow entrance. The captain slowed and studied the situation. He worried that a large wave might overtake the yacht as she entered and throw her against the breakwater, maybe even roll her over. But he knew waves came in cycles; after every seven or so big ones, a few smaller ones usually followed. He waited and counted. Then at what he thought was the best moment, he powered up the twin diesels for full speed and headed between the breakwaters, hoping to ride in on the face of an incoming swell. *Sequoia* swept pass the little Coast Guard station just inside the breakwater at what seemed like breakneck speed. Two "coasties" came out and stared as the yacht flew by, too surprised to even give her a wave.

Sequoia came to a halt inside the harbor close to where *Heaven Sent* was sounding her horn as her crew waved. The skipper of the sportfisherman called out, "Welcome to the town of Point Pleasant. The owner of that restaurant over yonder invites you to tie up at his dock." After *Sequoia* was tied up, the captain invited the owner aboard. He arrived with his staff bearing champagne for all hands. Soon after the celebration, television and newspaper reporters arrived to make the former presidential yacht the local celebrity of the day. The seas continued to pound the breakwater that night and all the next day before calming enough for *Sequoia* to make a safe exit for home.

Meanwhile back in Washington, R. Josh Lanier, who had been a successful "business crisis manager," was hired by the trust as executive director. Fundraising was soon intensified under his leadership. Cruises were arranged for disadvantaged children and for Special Olympics events. Young Naval Sea Cadets were invited aboard for hands-on training. Lanier encouraged the White House staff, the congressional leadership, and the cabinet to use the yacht, and they did.

The long-term goals of the trust began to focus on returning *Sequoia* to the government as a gift of the American people, although the U.S. Navy and White House officials made it quite clear that the yacht could only be accepted at no cost to taxpayers. Thus, the challenge for the trust was not only to raise funds to support the operations of the yacht and pay off debts, but also to endow the yacht for posterity. A tall order! The trust announced its goal was to raise $8 million by September 1988, at which time they expected to donate the yacht to the government fully endowed.

In 1983, the trust was promising donors of $5,000 or more they would be invited to private cruises at future dates. If the IRS or Coast Guard had any problem with that arrangement, it was apparently muted by congressional insistence that this historic yacht needed, and was worthy of, special privileges. Several of the trustees donated substantial personal funds to help support *Sequoia*. John Maguire, chairman of the trust, later estimated that by 1988 he had contributed about $4 million to the cause.

Sequoia provided hands-on training for Naval Sea Cadets. Courtesy Ann Stevens.

In the mid-1980s, *Sequoia* was often a venue for elegant dinner parties hosted by private individuals, associations, or senior government officials, and she again became a discreet meeting place for politicians and lobbyists. She was also the scene of birthday parties, prenuptial dinners, and even a wedding. Martin Sheen was on board to star in a promotional film about *Sequoia*. A big tent could be set up on her exclusive dock on Hains Point for large parties and dancing. At one such party Ginger Rogers was a guest of honor and was being shown around

Secretary of State George Shultz, *right,* with his guest British Foreign Secretary Sir Geoffrey Howe boarding *Sequoia* in 1986. *Left,* Chief of Protocol Selwa "Lucky" Roosevelt. Courtesy Ann Stevens.

the yacht by the captain. While descending from the upper deck, she caught her heel on the staircase and stumbled, but she was caught just in time to prevent a bad fall. When she recovered her composure, she turned to the captain with a charming smile and said, "Now sir, you and Fred Astaire have something in common. You have both caught me in your arms."

Among the government-sponsored cruises during the trust years were those hosted by Secretary of State George Shultz for British Foreign Secretary Sir Geoffrey Howe, and on May 20, 1987, by Vice President George Bush for Yang Shangkun just before he became president of China. For such state occasions *Sequoia* typically sailed to Mt. Vernon with two Secret Service agents aboard and two police boats as escorts. The agents, ever ready to lay down their lives to protect their charges, usually stationed themselves on the main deck, one on each side of the salon. Sometimes the agents stood on deck in the rain and cold. They could see their charges inside comfortably dining on fine cuisine by candlelight, while their dinner outside would be just sandwiches out of paper bags, sometimes seasoned with rain drops. Security was always tight.

The mid-1980s was something of a renaissance period for *Sequoia.* She entertained in high style and generated much interest and optimism about her future. Former Secretary of State Dean Rusk wrote: "I am very pleased that the good ship *Sequoia* is being returned to government hands and will be available to the presidency. [She] was a very useful adjunct to the presidency for purposes of entertaining and for receiving distinguished foreign guests. I was sad to see [her] go out of service."[2]

The Long Cruise of 1984: A Six-Thousand-Mile Odyssey

Motivated by both the need to raise substantial funds and a desire to share *Sequoia* and her history with as many people as practical, the Presidential Yacht Trust launched a national tour for the yacht in 1984, calling it "An American Odyssey." Along the waterways they expected the yacht would host fund-raisers and be present for local celebrations as she visited some forty ports in sixteen states.

Planning for this trip was extensive. A proposed itinerary was drawn up, then fleshed out by the trust after consulting with interested local contacts. The average daily cruise was projected to be about sixty-five miles with allowances for weather delays and an occasional day of rest for the crew. An important convenience was a van to follow the yacht's route and provide support on shore. Crew members would be assigned in turn by the captain to drive the van, do errands, pick up supplies, and be at that day's destination before the yacht arrived. The driver could then help to ensure that all arrangements were in order for mooring the yacht and receiving guests. A two-way radio in the van was ordered to provide the yacht with last-minute information about local conditions.

These arrangements would prove to work well. Typically a dock would be reserved for *Sequoia,* and a welcoming committee would greet the yacht. A press conference and photo opportunities could follow. Then the yacht would be open for visits by the public. The mayor or a local nonprofit organization was expected to sponsor a catered reception or dinner cruise with the objective of fund-raising.

Sequoia departed in early February for Florida, to have preliminary work for the tour done at the Huckins yard in Jacksonville before officially starting westward on the nation's inland waterways. A special addition to the yacht was a pair of presidential seals for her smokestack. *Sequoia* had not worn seals on her stack during her government service—merely life rings. An artisan on the staff of Marineland near St. Augustine, Florida, had seen the yacht when she wintered over there and offered to paint the seals on metal disks two feet in diameter. He presented them as a gift to the trust. With the impressive seals bolted in place on the stack, *Sequoia* was ready to show herself to the nation.

On April 1, 1984, seven years after President Carter had dispensed with

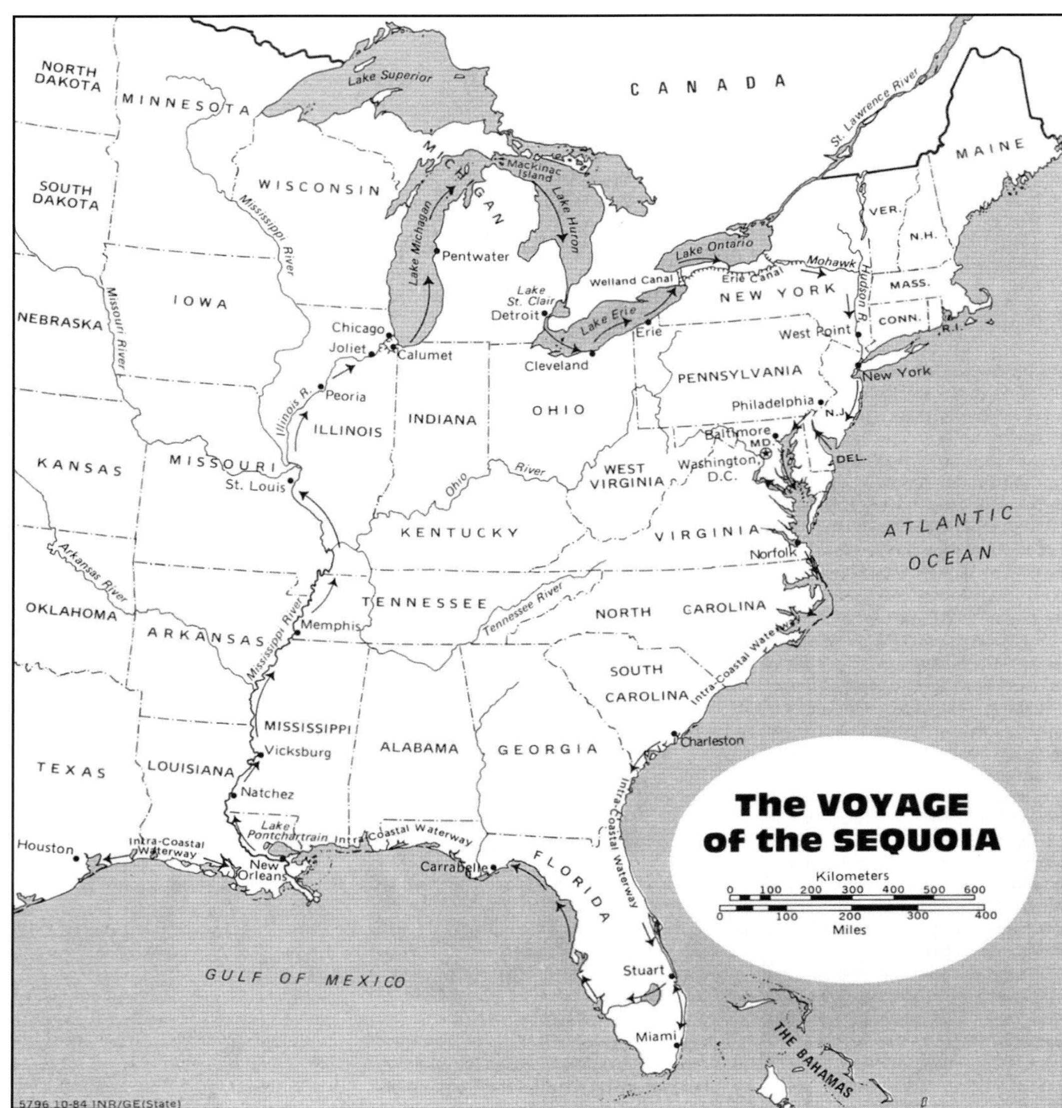

The route of the long cruise of 1984.

Sequoia, Susan Ford, daughter of the last president to use the yacht, cut the ribbon at St. Augustine, Florida, to send the yacht on a remarkable six-month, six-thousand-mile national goodwill cruise. Then the local band struck up a stirring march and dozens of colorful balloons were released into the sunny sky. *Sequoia* let go all lines and got underway.

Sequoia crossed Florida on the Okeechobee waterway to Fort Myers, then cruised up Florida's west coast, navigating along the Intracoastal Waterway to Clearwater. From there she sailed across

Executive Director Josh Lanier introducing Susan Ford, *seated at left,* who cut the ribbon to start the 1984 odyssey. Courtesy Ann Stevens.

a segment of the Gulf of Mexico to Apalachicola Bay on the Florida Panhandle. After reentering the Intracoastal Waterway there, she threaded her way along the Gulf Coast to Houston, Texas, where she was warmly welcomed by the mayor herself.

One moonless night while navigating the Kemah River near Houston with guests aboard, a memorable incident occurred. *Sequoia*'s sensitive radar picked up an object moving slowly across her bow, but nothing could be seen ahead on the dark waters, even with binoculars.

The captain, concerned that there might be a canoeist, a swimmer, or a small boat out there, stopped the yacht

Seals to be displayed on *Sequoia*'s stack were among the many gifts received in 1984. Courtesy Ann Stevens.

Sequoia making her way toward Natchez, Mississippi. Courtesy Ann Stevens.

and ordered the searchlight turned on. It illuminated a mother duck followed by six little ducklings paddling double-time across the river. Of course they were given the right-of-way.

After visiting Houston, *Sequoia* reversed course and headed to New Orleans to start the second leg of her journey. That leg took her up the Mississippi River in May to St. Louis, then along the Illinois River to the Chicago River, and a passage through the busy heart of Chicago to moor at Navy Pier on Lake Michigan. However, on the way she was blocked at Peoria, Illinois, by a low railroad bridge that no longer opened. To get under it required removing *Sequoia*'s stack, mast and awnings from the upper deck. A mobile crane was called in to lift off these parts, then replace them once *Sequoia* was on the other side of the bridge.

Throughout this long cruise *Sequoia* was well-received at every port. Sometimes flotillas of pleasure boats appeared to escort her to her dock. Often crowds and sometimes bands greeted her as she visited Great Lakes ports. People were curious to see the yacht of presidents and eager to walk on her main deck. They were thrilled to see her salon set for a presidential dinner party with gleaming silver and crystal and a beautiful centerpiece of fresh flowers. There was never a charge for such public visits; however, donations were often offered and welcomed for the preservation of the yacht.

In the after salon, visitors closely studied the photographs of various presidents on board *Sequoia.* Many visitors seemed to sense they were viewing history, and they were in awe. Some had tears in their eyes upon seeing the poignant photos of President Kennedy and his friends enjoying his birthday party—his last—on board. A frequent comment was: "This is quite a small yacht for a superpower," but the most frequently asked question was, "Why did Jimmy Carter sell her?"

Sequoia called at small Michigan ports such as Grand Haven, Pentwater, and Mackinac Island. She also was celebrated at Detroit and Cleveland. Midwestern visitors particularly seemed to appreciate *Sequoia* as a unique icon of the American presidency. The farther she was from Washington, the more enthusiasm she seemed to inspire. Perhaps that was because in the heartland, things closely associated with the presidency are not often seen so close-up.

Sequoia even visited a bit of Canada as she passed through the locks of the Welland Canal, which lowered the yacht from Lake Erie into Lake Ontario on her way to Oswego, New York. There she entered the feeder canal leading to the New York State Barge Canal (Erie Canal) and the Mohawk River. *Sequoia* crossed New York State to reach the Hudson River at Albany, then sailed down the Hudson, visiting West Point and mooring at Governors Island in New York harbor.

Near Peoria, Illinois, parts of *Sequoia*'s superstructure were removed to enable her to pass under a fixed bridge. This operation had to be repeated later for a low bridge at Oswego, New York. Courtesy Ann Stevens.

Heading home, the yacht ran smoothly enough along the coast of New Jersey to the Delaware Bay and from there entered the Chesapeake Bay via the C and D canal. On her return to Washington, D.C., in September 1984, she was greeted by a Dixieland band and a personal welcome home from Washington's colorful mayor Marion Barry. By then *Sequoia* had been seen by thousands of people during her six-month odyssey. Local television and newspaper coverage

Visitors formed long lines to visit the presidential yacht. This line was in St. Joseph, Michigan, at the beginning of *Sequoia*'s swing through the Great Lakes. Courtesy Ann Stevens.

A welcoming committee turned out to greet *Sequoia* at Pentwater, Michigan, in 1984. Courtesy Giles Kelly.

Sequoia negotiating the locks of Canada's Welland Canal. Courtesy Ann Stevens.

along the way had been extensive. She had been hailed everywhere as an American treasure.[3]

After inspired lobbying by the trust and with the support of Senators Alan Simpson of Wyoming, Jake Garn of Utah, and Alan Cranston of California, a joint resolution was passed in the Congress. It began:

> We believe this resolution, endorsing the return of *Sequoia* to government service, is an important step in assuring continued private financial support of the endowment fund and public awareness of this important project.

The Joint Resolution of December 16, 1985, went on to state in part:

> That Congress (1) recognizes the unique significance of the former Presidential yacht *Sequoia* which has made her a symbol of American political heritage and the Office of the President; (2)

Sequoia passing the Battery, New York City. Courtesy Ann Stevens.

> supports the plans of the Presidential Yacht Trust to donate the *Sequoia,* with an endowment sufficient for operations and maintenance, to the United States Navy for service once again as the Presidential yacht."[4]

President Reagan still showed no interest in visiting—let alone using—*Sequoia,* perhaps feeling that when money was short for education and welfare projects, it was no time for him to be associated with a yacht. Or perhaps it was just that he preferred to ride on a horse rather than a yacht. In any case, this was a great disappointment to the trustees, as they felt the president's endorsement was essential to the success of their fund-raising.

Major Restoration and Afterward, 1986–87

> When I started working on this project, I was doing it as a kind of patriotic duty, and that still holds, but now that I know this ship, and have learned to love her, I think I'm doing it for her. She's such a great ship.
>
> —John Maguire, Chairman, Presidential Yacht Trust, 1985

Buoyed by the public enthusiasm seen on the long cruise and by the support in Congress for return of the yacht to the government, the trust sent *Sequoia* in February 1986 to the Norfolk Shipbuilding and Dry Dock Company (Norshipco), a Norfolk, Virginia, ship repair yard with the facilities and know-how to repair wooden boats. The trust's orders to the captain and to the executive director were simply, "Do what is necessary to get her ready for presidential use." No specific budget was set for the work. Credits and loans were arranged under the chairmanship of John Maguire. Repayment was envisioned through a two-year fund-raising campaign to begin in the summer of 1986.

In June the Reagan White House finally got around to issuing a supporting statement entitled "The Preservation and Return of the Former Presidential Yacht *Sequoia*." It recognized the yacht as one of the most historic vessels in America. It noted that tens of thousands of Americans had the unique opportunity to visit her and demonstrate support for her preservation during her 1984 national tour, and that the trust, in consultation with the Naval Historical Foundation, had recently determined the proper future role for *Sequoia* would be her return to the United States Navy. It stated, "The President joins with the Congress in both recognizing the unique historical significance of the *Sequoia* and in supporting the plans for her preservation and return to official service without expense to the American taxpayers."[5]

Two of the most annoying, even embarrassing, problems with the yacht were the porous upper deck that allowed rainwater to drip into the main salon and into the lower reaches of the hull, eating away at the planking and frames. Seventy of

Seventy percent of *Sequoia*'s planks were replaced during her 1986 restoration. Courtesy Ann Stevens.

her ninety-five frames had to be bolstered and more than half of her planking had to be replaced. The air-conditioning system had proven inadequate and had to be upgraded. Sixty-five craftsmen went to work on her. Her upper and main decks were both renewed. The upper deck was raised by four inches to give the main salon a bit more headroom for a taller generation.

While the decks were being replaced, it was the ideal time to install new engines and higher capacity generators. That opportunity was not missed. Her twin Gray Marine 6-71 diesel engines were replaced with the more powerful 8-71 diesels. Two new 50-kilowatt generators were installed to carry the greater loads needed for more

New engines and generators were installed in 1986. Courtesy Ann Stevens.

effective air-conditioning and for the new all-electric galley that would include added refrigeration, an ice maker, a dumbwaiter, and electric stoves. A new smokestack was fabricated out of aluminum.

Kissinger's complaint about the engine noise was not forgotten. Sound insulation was given special attention. Giant exhaust mufflers were installed, and all exhaust gases were emitted underwater. The engine room was fully soundproofed. All bathrooms were fitted with the latest electric flushing toilets. Video cameras were fitted so the engine room, the main salon, and the view astern could all be monitored from the pilothouse. A modern security system and a fire suppression system were installed, as was a new gyrocompass and a high-quality sound system. Many new furnishings were purchased. Among the most impressive was a fitted carpet for the main salon, showing a woven-in presidential seal.

Generous donations were received from the marine industry to provide new equipment ranging from rugs to radar. The list of donors and donations was impressive. For example, the Sperry Corporation donated and installed a gyrocompass and a secondary radar. B.F. Goodrich donated two life rafts, and Dean Hardwoods Inc. of Wilmington, North Carolina, supplied teak and other fine woods. The Koppers Company provided paints and varnishes, and Electrolux gave a carpet-care system. Many American businesses, large and small, showed they were ready to support the restoration and enhancement of the yacht.

At the start of the restoration work, the trust was told by the yard that the work would cost about $1 million. But later, when the trust decided the work had to be done in time for the yacht to participate in the July 4, 1986, centennial celebration of the Statue of Liberty, two shifts were put on the job to hasten completion. The work continued day and night between January and June 1986 to finish in time. That overtime ran the cost up to more than $2 million, with dire consequences.

The skill and enthusiasm of the Norshipco workers was impressive. They

Sequoia's upper deck was raised four inches and renewed during her 1986 restoration. Courtesy Ann Stevens.

Stern view showing *Sequoia's* double-winged rudder and her "ducktail" under her stern. Courtesy Ann Stevens.

seemed proud to work on such a historic wooden yacht. When the restoration was completed on time, June 15, 1986, one of the yard workers said, "I don't want to wish you any ill luck, Captain, but we like working on this old yacht and hope there will be reason for you to bring her back real soon."

On hand in Norfolk to celebrate the completion of the restoration work were U.S. Senator Alan Simpson, Under Secretary of the Navy James Goodrich, and three of *Sequoia*'s retired former skippers—Captain Andrew Combs, Captain Arthur Ismay, and Captain "Tex" Winslow. Speeches were made, a band played, and two huge cakes were served to workers and visitors. The renewed *Sequoia* indeed looked ready in all respects on that day for presidential use.

Sequoia promptly sailed to New York harbor, where Secretary of Commerce William Brock and several leading members of Congress came on board. President Reagan was embarked on the great gray battleship *Iowa*. As she steamed down the Hudson River for the review of the assembled tall ships, she was escorted by *Sequoia*. From *Sequoia*'s decks, an ABC crew televised the scene as hundreds of yachts, warships, and tall ships assembled against the background of the newly restored Statue of Liberty.

That night after the fireworks, *Sequoia* retired to the security of the New

The new carpet in the main salon features the presidential seal. The cakes were ordered to help celebrate completion of the restoration. In the background, crew member and steward Ben Alger awaits drink orders. Courtesy Ann Stevens.

Ann Simpson, wife of Senator Alan Simpson, cut the ribbon marking the completion of *Sequoia*'s restoration. Looking on, *left to right,* are Chairman of the Trust John Maguire, Senator Simpson, two Norshipco supervisors, and Undersecretary of the Navy James Goodrich. Courtesy Ann Stevens.

York Shipyard in Brooklyn along with several megayachts. Next morning the crew was shocked to find that both of the presidential seals bolted to her stack were missing—they'd been stolen! The yacht suddenly seemed naked without those distinctive emblems that had quickly become her trademark. Replacement seals were made over the summer, while *Sequoia* cruised on Long Island Sound. She visited the U.S. Merchant Marine Academy at Kings Point and several venerable yacht clubs on the Sound, including Larchmont (New York) Yacht Club and Indian Harbor Yacht Club at Greenwich, Connecticut. She also participated as the honored guest in a regatta of antique wooden boats at Mystic Seaport in Connecticut.

That fall, when the giant nuclear carrier USS *Theodore Roosevelt* was ready to be put into commission, the commanding officer of *Roosevelt* asked if *Sequoia* could be present at the ceremony in Newport News, Virginia. On October 25, 1986, *Sequoia* tied up to a decorated and tented barge positioned across the stern of the towering carrier. She was on a special mission which could be helpful to the navy.

It is well known that navy ships are dry, but not so *Sequoia*. Under Presidential Yacht Trust ownership, she could be well stocked for any occasion. When the commissioning ceremony was over, *Roosevelt*'s commanding officer was thus able to invite his guests of honor to proceed across the barge astern and board the former presidential yacht for a champagne toast to the new warship. President Teddy Roosevelt would have approved. The elegant little wooden yacht, dwarfed by the big carrier that afternoon, received on board the secretary of defense, the chairman of the joint chiefs of staff, the secretary of the navy, the national security advisor, the chief of naval operations, and a covey of senior admirals. Once again she proved to be well up to her mission of providing quality hospitality to VIPs.

The next day a message received aboard *Sequoia* from the *Roosevelt* read: "*Sequoia*'s presence added immeasurably to the dignity and grace of the occasion. All in attendance were impressed by the smartness of the vessel and the professionalism of her crew." A few months later a lieutenant from USS *Theodore Roosevelt,* who must have been well impressed by *Sequoia,* asked to have his formal wedding ceremony on board her in Washington. Permission was granted.

During the summer of 1987, *Sequoia*'s condition and history were reviewed by National Park Service officials James P. Delgado and Kevin J. Foster, who recommended to the secretary of the interior that *Sequoia* be designated a National Historic Landmark. She was officially so designated in March 1988.

At the onset of winter in 1987, *Sequoia* once again was headed south on the Intracoastal Waterway to Florida, stopping each night along the way at marinas, where for the most part she was offered a free berth as a sort of symbolic vote for her continued preservation. Such late fall trips were not easy because of the heavy fogbanks that often covered the coastline and blanked out the narrow channels of the waterway. Under such hazardous conditions, navigating the intricate waterway could be continued in *Sequoia* only by virtue of the large ship-sized radar console on board that had been donated by the Raytheon Corporation.

Admiral William J. Crowe, chairman of the joint chiefs of staff, examining a historic photo with the author aboard *Sequoia* after the carrier's commissioning. Courtesy Ann Stevens.

The fact that many of the guests who cruised aboard *Sequoia* were well over seventy years old was a concern to the captain. During a cruise one of these guests might have a medical emergency. Besides keeping an oxygen bottle on hand, he felt the crew should have some paramedical training to deal with such an emergency. When *Sequoia* was scheduled to sail from Washington in October 1987 on the twelve-day trip to her winter quar-

Sequoia moored astern of the USS *Theodore Roosevelt* to host VIPs after the commissioning of the giant carrier. Courtesy Ann Stevens.

ters in Florida, he asked Robert Barnes, a retired doctor, to join the crew as the "medical officer" and give lessons for handling medical emergencies. As usual on such long distance cruises, *Sequoia* was accompanied by a van, driven in turns by crew members, to provide support along the way for emergencies and do ordinary errands.

That year *Sequoia* moored just south of St. Augustine, Florida, as a guest at Marineland, where she had a protected berth surrounded by royal palms and lawns fringed with bougainvillea. Visitors to Marineland could watch the crew touching up the paint and varnish, a never-ending job.

Failure of the Trust, 1988

At the outset, the idea to give the former presidential yacht back to the government early in 1987 had bipartisan backing in Congress. Republican Senator Alan Simpson was *Sequoia*'s chief congressional sponsor. Frank Fahrenkopf, chairman of the Republican National Committee, and Paul Kirk, chairman of the Democratic National Committee, signed on as honorary cochairmen of the

Sequoia was the site for a naval military wedding. Courtesy Ann Stevens.

trust's Transition Committee. Even former President Carter supported the idea, writing to the trust at the time that: "This is good news to presidents and U.S. taxpayers." However, the navy was not fully "on board."

Beginning in August of 1987, at the request of the vice chief of naval operations, the navy began to look into the physical and financial implications of the proposal. When studies were made, opinions surfaced that the costs of maintenance, operations, and providing security would be well beyond the means of the trust's proposed endowment. Thus there would be a residual cost to the navy. Making up the shortfall from the navy budget and manning the yacht with a naval crew raised concerns that such an arrangement would be viewed by the public as misuse of navy personnel and funds better used for the fleet. The navy had recently been stung by public criticism for using navy personnel to man the frigate USS *Constitution*. However, the navy recognized the *Sequoia* matter was politically sensitive and cautiously held its fire to see how far Congress and the White House would go with the idea.

Meanwhile, during the winter of 1987–88, the Presidential Yacht Trust planned a second tour for *Sequoia* similar to the national tour of 1984. This time the purpose was to raise serious funds for the endowment and to complete payments for the restoration work done in 1986. This tour was to be called "Celebrate America." But to send the newly renovated yacht again up the Mississippi River and through the Great Lakes for that purpose (rather than, for example, visits along the closer and more affluent East Coast) seemed to some observers a poor allocation of time and resources. They feared that a repeat of the long and difficult trip of 1984 would expose the yacht to unnecessary risks and would not raise the needed funds. Her captain resigned over the matter and John Terrill, the mate who had served aboard for two years, was appointed the new skipper.

In preparation for the "Celebrate America" cruise, the trust managed to obtain a $2.3 million loan from the National Bank of Washington, even though the trust was still heavily in debt to the Norfolk shipyard. With the new money in hand Lanier increased his three-person staff to eleven people including public relations personnel and an advance team for the cruise. He also moved the trust office to a suite in the high-rent district of downtown Washington. As the 1988 cruise began in May, the trust drew up plans for the grand finale in Washington at the end of the summer, to be followed by a ceremonial turnover of the yacht to the navy in November. That July Navy Yard personnel met with Secret Service representatives to work out security details for the yacht which would include twenty-four-hour surveillance and installation of an elaborate physical barrier around the berthing slip.[6]

Meanwhile, the secretary of defense wrote to the president, noting the trust was currently raising funds to turn over the yacht to the navy, but stating that the amount of funds proposed by the trust would not be sufficient without some expense to the taxpayer. However, he assured the president the navy would work with the White House and the trust to develop an arrangement under which the navy would accept and operate *Sequoia* at a minimum of taxpayer expense.[7]

While the cruise was underway, the navy's concerns increased over the prospect of becoming owner of the yacht as more cost estimates were drawn up, with negative implications. The trust, meanwhile, was having a hard time raising the funds it needed for the endowment; as a result it proposed the turnover date be moved from November 1988 to April 1989 to provide more time. That suited the navy just fine, because the delay gave more lead time that would be needed to install the infrastructure required for security of a presidential yacht at the Navy Yard.

But nothing turned out as envisioned. Although the cruise went safely enough, so little money was raised and so much money was spent that the trust ran short of funds even before the yacht could return to Washington. The crew reported waiting days at Sandy Hook, New Jersey, for funds to buy enough fuel to get back to Washington. By the time *Sequoia* did return home, plans for her future had fallen apart. The trust had defaulted on its loan and was near bankruptcy. When the bank notified the political backers of the yacht of the situation, Fahrenkopf and Kirk pulled out of the trust, saying they didn't want to have anything more to do with the yacht. Presumably the navy was much relieved.

According to the *Wall Street Journal,* documents demanded by concerned congressional leaders revealed the trust had amassed a debt of nearly $10 million and had raised less than $1.5 million. Senator Simpson said, "It is a disappointment. . . . To me it was a great idea." A bailout by Congress was suggested and considered, but turned down. The bank sued Chairman of the Trust John Maguire and Executive Director Josh Lanier for misrepresentation when they negotiated for the $2.3 million loan. Maguire, who had already put $4 million into the project said, "I've learned a very expensive lesson."[8]

Thus, all bets were off, and the navy's problems with the transfer became moot. It was a sad climax to the great efforts and noble plans of the trust. When the yacht quietly arrived back in Washington, she was sent on to Norfolk, Virginia, for safekeeping at Norshipco. The crew was then dismissed, and the yacht laid up.

Further efforts by the trust failed to raise funds to relieve the debt to Norshipco. *Sequoia* was put up for auction by court order in July 1989. Norshipco was still owed well over a million dollars for the work they had done on her in 1986. As they were the only bidders for the yacht, they acquired title for a mere $50,000. Late in 1989, they had a professional appraisal done. Given her Trumpy pedigree and the presidential overlay, the ship was appraised at $3.2 million. However, Norshipco simply stored *Sequoia* in a covered wet slip in Norfolk where she remained idle for the next six years.

CHAPTER EIGHT

Seeking a Course for *Sequoia*, 1998–2004

The original quality construction and her easy use in protected waters have allowed [Sequoia] *to age gracefully.*

—U.S. Coast Guard Inspector Commander Mark Cruder

When the first Gulf War was over in 1991, former Presidential Yacht Trust Executive Director Josh Lanier and E. R. Carlisle, a retired vice president from Norshipco, flew to Kuwait in an effort to persuade the Kuwaiti government to express its appreciation to President Bush for the American war effort by purchasing *Sequoia* and donating her with an endowment to the U.S. government. However, the Kuwaiti government did not buy the idea, and the yacht remained in storage in Norfolk.[1]

In the late 1990s, Norshipco took several initiatives with the yacht. They encouraged a volunteer crew to dust her off and display her at a festival in Jamestown, Virginia, where she drew crowds. Reportedly, the shipyard also asked Sotheby auctioneers to again put up *Sequoia* for sale, but they declined.

Sequoia Refurbished, Certified, and Sold in 2000

Norshipco believed *Sequoia* would be more salable if she could be operated commercially, but to do so, she needed a Coast Guard certificate that would allow her to carry paying passengers. However, since she had been designated a National Historic Landmark back in 1989, there would be major problems meeting normal Coast Guard safety requirements, such as changing her structure to install watertight doors and bulkheads. Norshipco sought and obtained special legislation from Congress in 1995 that would exempt *Sequoia* from certain Coast Guard regulations. For example, *Sequoia* was deemed to be less than 100 tons for regulatory purposes (instead of her 133 actual net tons). Certain requirements in the

Naval Sea Cadets train aboard *Sequoia* by providing side honors for VIP guests and helping with classic polishing duties. Courtesy Naval Sea Cadets, Dahlgren Division.

United States Code also could be waived at the discretion of the secretary of transportation (in effect, by the U.S. Coast Guard), thereby excusing the yacht from regulations that would have degraded her historic integrity.

Nevertheless, some alterations were required. *Sequoia*'s handrails had to be raised six inches for passenger safety; she was required to carry more life rafts and have a minimum number and type of crew members on board when carrying paying passengers. Also, limits were imposed on where she could operate as a charter vessel. She was restricted to sheltered waters and to carrying no more than forty-nine passengers. After some $400,000 worth of upgrades followed by a close inspection by the Coast Guard, she qualified in 1997 for a special certificate but was required to be reinspected out of water every two years.

Once certified, the yard loaned out *Sequoia* during two boating seasons to two separate nonprofit organizations. One of these "borrowers" took the yacht to Washington, D.C., and the other to Annapolis, Maryland, both intending to raise money through charters to pay for her operations. They also hoped to raise funds for eventual purchase of the yacht. However, both organizations barely succeeded in raising enough funds for her current operations and maintenance. They also found it quite impractical to raise capital funds toward purchasing the yacht, despite the availability of a tax deduction for donors, without first having in hand an exclusive purchase agreement with the owners, which they failed to get.

While the yacht was on loan during the summer of 1998, she was allowed to berth at the Washington Navy Yard. This was permitted only because *Sequoia* had been designated a historic vessel and at the time was being operated by a nonprofit organization. While she was in Washington, a minor historical event took place. Secretary of the Navy John Dalton borrowed *Sequoia* in June for an evening cruise with senior government officials and their wives. It was the first time in twenty-two years that the secretary of the navy's flag was flown aboard *Sequoia*. The navy's interest in the yacht has continued—if her use by Secretary of the Navy Gordon England is any indication. He borrowed her to celebrate Navy and Marine Corps Day in 2002 and again in 2004 for diplomatic entertaining of Egyptian senior officials.

Other navy interest in *Sequoia* also had been expressed in an April 1999 letter from the commandant of the Naval District of Washington, Rear Admiral Christopher Weaver, to Lieutenant Commander "Hank" Mooberry, commanding officer of the U.S. Naval Sea Cadet Division imbedded at the Navy Yard. The admiral wrote in part: ". . . accept my assurance that all reasonable efforts will be made to facilitate the return of *Sequoia* . . . with a clear understanding of her important role here at the Navy Yard." He was referring to *Sequoia* having had a popular training program in the 1980s for the Naval Sea Cadet unit at the Navy Yard.

In October 1999 the shipyard that owned *Sequoia*, Norshipco, was bought by Southwest Marine. Shortly afterwards the new owners put *Sequoia* up for sale. The advertised price was $2.5 million, but there were no buyers at that price.[2] However, in August 2000, Gary Silversmith, a Washington, D.C., lawyer, investor, and collector of presidential memorabilia, bought *Sequoia* for $1.9 million. He brought her to Washington and embellished her with his collection of presidential memorabilia making her into a virtual museum. Anthony Wells was appointed skipper, and the yacht was made available for four-hour charters at the rate of $10,000.

Sequoia, shy of most of her traditional canvas, shown moored at the commercial dock of the Gangplank Marina in Washington, D.C., in 2003. Courtesy Giles Kelly.

Early in Silversmith's ownership of *Sequoia,* President William Clinton visited the yacht as a guest of a congresswoman who had chartered the yacht for an evening party. Thus on October 17, 2000, Clinton became the eighth president while in office to enjoy *Sequoia,* joining his predecessors: Hoover, Roosevelt, Truman, Kennedy, Johnson, Nixon, and Ford. The first George Bush was aboard, but only when he was vice president, and Eisenhower was on board, but only when he was army chief of staff. Carter and Reagan were never on board. It seems unlikely Clinton will be the last White House occupant to enjoy this modest yacht already loaded with a "cargo of presidential history."

During Wells's stewardship of *Sequoia* between 2000 and 2003, he made many trips on the Potomac River. Wells especially likes to tell about former General Secretary of the Soviet Union Mikhail Gorbachev being on board in 2001 as the guest of honor. Gorbachev came up to the wheelhouse and insisted on taking the helm because, he said, "I have always dreamed of being in charge of the 'American ship of state.'"

Operating *Sequoia* as a commercial venture with few full-time crew members was criticized by some mariners and historians as inappropriate for this antique wooden vessel with a proud presidential past. Even the *New York Times,* in an editorial in 2003, said that "*[Sequoia]* ought to be in a safer place where it can be revered rather than rented."[3]

Nevertheless, Silversmith kept *Sequoia* operational and in the public eye. The History Channel featured the yacht in an hour-long television review of her history that was first aired in 2003. That same year National Public Radio's Susan Stamberg devoted a segment of *Morning Edition* to describing the look and the history of the yacht. *Sequoia* also was mentioned frequently in the Style Section of the *Washington Post* in connection with parties held on board. In 2003 Silversmith made *Sequoia* available for a reunion of her former navy crew members for a celebration cruise on the Potomac River.

Interest in *Sequoia*'s future rose as she entered still intact into the new century. More people recognized that her historic importance merits preservation rather than exploitation. With Silversmith's encouragement, several nonprofit organization attempted to raise funds from private and government sources to purchase, preserve, and endow her so she could be available for special uses, including government duty, ceremonial events, and training. Suggestions also were made to associate her with one of the maritime museums, the navy museum, or the Smithsonian Institution. However, as this book went to press, none of these ideas had been realized. Apparently no organization had met the owner's asking price for her, but the quest for money and new ideas for *Sequoia* continued.

A Salute to the Coast Guard

The *Sequoia* story is not complete without a salute to the U.S. Coast Guard. *Sequoia* has been able to "sail on" in no

The Coast Guard cutter *Legare* was a sister ship of *Cuyahoga* (circa 1933) that was used to escort *Sequoia* during Roosevelt's administration. Courtesy U.S. Coast Guard.

small part due to the support given to her by the Coast Guard over the years. An almost symbiotic relationship began in 1931 when both *Sequoia* and the cutter *Kilkenny* were owned by the U.S. Department of Commerce. When President Hoover first used *Sequoia, Kilkenny* was assigned as her escort. At that time both vessels were assigned to the Bureau of Marine Inspection and Navigation. The responsibilities of that bureau were transferred in 1942 to the Coast Guard.

When *Sequoia* became the official presidential yacht for Roosevelt in 1933, the 125-foot Coast Guard cutter *Cuyahoga* was assigned as her escort. Early Coast Guard support also included, occasionally, provision of an amphibious plane to deliver President Roosevelt's guests to *Sequoia* when he was cruising on the Chesapeake Bay.

During the presidential years of Johnson, Nixon, and Ford, a detachment of ten coast guardsmen with three fast 25-foot Coast Guard patrol boats were assigned to the Administrative Unit at Washington Navy Yard to work with the Secret Service to provide security for the presidential yacht. They kept the channel clear ahead for the yacht and were prepared to take the president ashore in an emergency. Andrew Combe, skipper of *Sequoia* during the Nixon years, said these Coast Guard boats were also used as tugs to help dock *Sequoia* in high winds.

Some of the "coasties," as they were affectionately known, assigned to the Naval Administrative Unit not only ran the escort boats, but also served on board *Sequoia* as watch standers. Combe said several Coast Guard petty officers qualified as "yacht captains," a term meaning they were qualified to pilot *Sequoia*.

Years later when *Sequoia* was in private ownership, the Coast Guard was asked to issue an "attraction vessel certificate," a special document that would allow her to carry paying passengers. As previously noted, *Sequoia* could not otherwise meet all the normal safety requirements to qualify as a commercial vessel. The special certificate was issued in 1997 in deference to *Sequoia*'s historical integrity, which precluded making radical alterations, and in recognition of the need for *Sequoia* to continue to earn her keep.

U.S. Coast Guard Inspector Commander Mark Cruder put it this way in his official report:

> The *Sequoia* is listed as a national treasure by the National Trust for Historic Preservation. As a result of this status and the need to operate commercially to maintain the vessel, special legislation was sought . . . from the Congress that provided the vessel M/V *Sequoia* is deemed (for section 1132 of Title 46 of the *U.S. Code*) to be less than 100 gross tons and the Secretary of Transportation may exempt that vessel from certain requirements of section 3306 of Title 46 *U.S. Code,* and the regulations thereunder. The Secretary may impose special operating restrictions on that vessel as to route, service, manning and

The fast Coast Guard boats that escorted *Sequoia* in 1973. Official White House photo, courtesy Andrew Combe.

equipment, necessary for the safe operation of that vessel.

Over many years the U.S. Coast Guard has been a guardian of *Sequoia* both afloat and ashore. The Coast Guard has found practical ways to balance safety considerations with her historic preservation. Officials have gone out of their way to help keep *Sequoia* operational. Without the Coast Guard's continuous interest in her safety and integrity, it is doubtful *Sequoia* would have sailed so well into the twenty-first century.

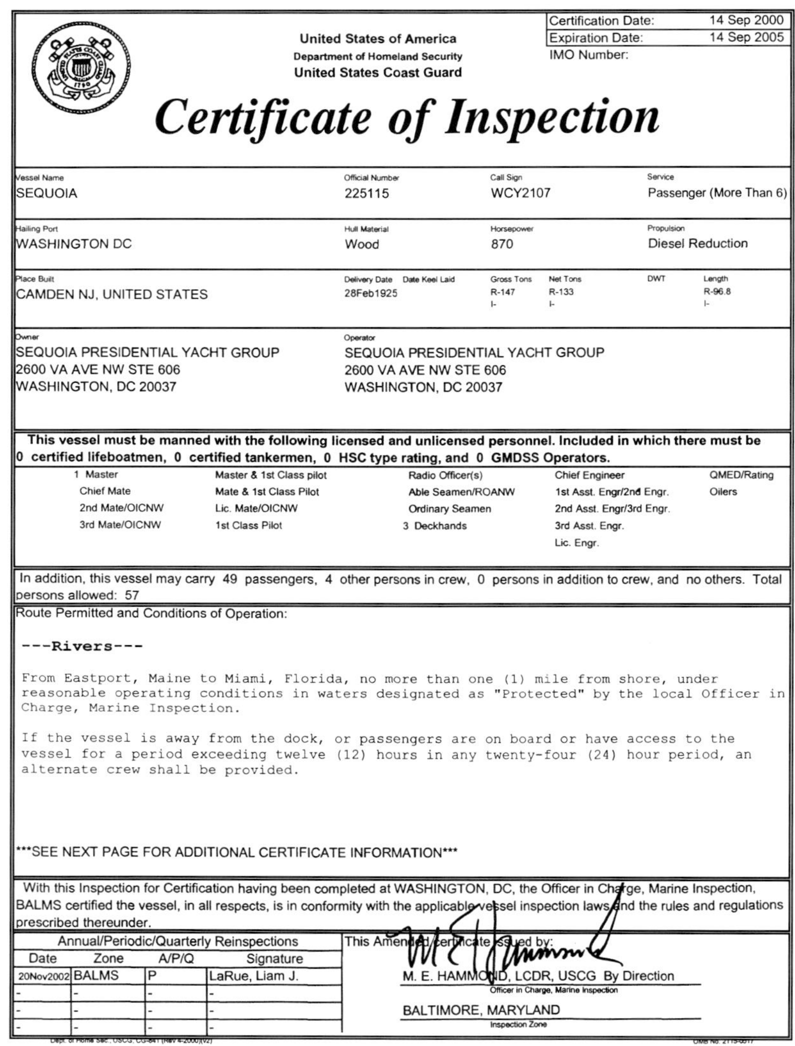

United States of America
Department of Homeland Security
United States Coast Guard

Certification Date: 14 Sep 2000
Expiration Date: 14 Sep 2005
IMO Number:

Certificate of Inspection

Vessel Name	Official Number	Call Sign	Service
SEQUOIA	225115	WCY2107	Passenger (More Than 6)

Hailing Port	Hull Material	Horsepower	Propulsion
WASHINGTON DC	Wood	870	Diesel Reduction

Place Built	Delivery Date	Date Keel Laid	Gross Tons	Net Tons	DWT	Length
CAMDEN NJ, UNITED STATES	28Feb1925		R-147 I-	R-133 I-		R-96.8 I-

Owner	Operator
SEQUOIA PRESIDENTIAL YACHT GROUP 2600 VA AVE NW STE 606 WASHINGTON, DC 20037	SEQUOIA PRESIDENTIAL YACHT GROUP 2600 VA AVE NW STE 606 WASHINGTON, DC 20037

This vessel must be manned with the following licensed and unlicensed personnel. Included in which there must be 0 certified lifeboatmen, 0 certified tankermen, 0 HSC type rating, and 0 GMDSS Operators.

1 Master	Master & 1st Class pilot	Radio Officer(s)	Chief Engineer	QMED/Rating
Chief Mate	Mate & 1st Class Pilot	Able Seamen/ROANW	1st Asst. Engr/2nd Engr.	Oilers
2nd Mate/OICNW	Lic. Mate/OICNW	Ordinary Seamen	2nd Asst. Engr/3rd Engr.	
3rd Mate/OICNW	1st Class Pilot	3 Deckhands	3rd Asst. Engr.	
			Lic. Engr.	

In addition, this vessel may carry 49 passengers, 4 other persons in crew, 0 persons in addition to crew, and no others. Total persons allowed: 57

Route Permitted and Conditions of Operation:

---Rivers---

From Eastport, Maine to Miami, Florida, no more than one (1) mile from shore, under reasonable operating conditions in waters designated as "Protected" by the local Officer in Charge, Marine Inspection.

If the vessel is away from the dock, or passengers are on board or have access to the vessel for a period exceeding twelve (12) hours in any twenty-four (24) hour period, an alternate crew shall be provided.

SEE NEXT PAGE FOR ADDITIONAL CERTIFICATE INFORMATION

With this Inspection for Certification having been completed at WASHINGTON, DC, the Officer in Charge, Marine Inspection, BALMS certified the vessel, in all respects, is in conformity with the applicable vessel inspection laws and the rules and regulations prescribed thereunder.

Annual/Periodic/Quarterly Reinspections			
Date	Zone	A/P/Q	Signature
20Nov2002	BALMS	P	LaRue, Liam J.
-	-	-	-
-	-	-	-
-	-	-	-

This Amended certificate issued by:

M. E. HAMMOND, LCDR, USCG By Direction
Officer in Charge, Marine Inspection

BALTIMORE, MARYLAND
Inspection Zone

Sequoia's 2004 Certificate of Inspection with conditions of operation.

Appendix

Excerpt from Lloyd's Register of American Yachts (1926) Showing *Sequoia* and *Sequoia II*

LIST OF YACHTS OF THE UNITED STATES AND CANADA

1 Annual No.	2 Yacht's Name. Former Names.	Build.	3 Hull-Type. Rig. Sailmaker. Sails made. Sail area.	4 Register. Official Number. Signal Letters.	Tons. Net. Gross.	5 Dimensions in feet and inches. Length. O. A. W. L.	Extreme Breadth.	Depth. Draft.	6 Design and Build. Designer. Builder. Place and Date of Launch.	7 Machinery. Description. Dimensions. Build.	8 Owner.	9 Home Port. Port of Registry.	10 Classification. Character. Port of Survey ✠ for Special Survey. Date of Last Survey.
2897	Sequoia	Wood	K DC Pwr Twn	224073 MFPR	77 91	85– 0 79–10	17– 2	8– 2 3– 9	Mathis Yacht Building Co. Mathis Yacht Building Co. Camden, N. J. 1924	Gas Eng. 4 Cyc. 6 Cyl. 5¼×7 Speedway	Richard M. Cadwalader	Essington, Pa. Philadelphia	
2898	Sequoia II	Wood	K DC Pwr Twn *	225115 MFTS	133 147	104– 7 98–11	19– 0	6– 6 4– 4	Mathis Yacht Building Co. Mathis Yacht Building Co. Camden, N. J. 1925	2 Gas Eng. 4 Cyc. 6 Cyl. 7½×8½ Winton	Richard M. Cadwalader	Essington, Pa. Philadelphia	
2899	Serene Halcyon	Wood	Cb TC Aux Ywl		—	40– 0 30– 0	12– 6	— 3– 6	Clinton Sturges Clinton Sturges Hyannis Port, Mass.	Gas Eng. 4 Cyc. 2 Cyl. 6×8 Standard 1913	W. S. Galloway	Baltimore Md.	
2900	Serene III	Wood	K TC Pwr		—	24– 0 23– 0	7– 0	— 2– 6	Navy Dept. U. S. A. Navy Dept. U. S. A.	Gas Eng. 4 Cyc. 2 Cyl. 5×6 Palmer	John W. Sherwood	Annapolis, Md.	
2901	Serenity	Wood	K RD Pwr	210126	13 17	43– 0 42– 0	9– 5	7– 4 2–10	J. Murray Watts Salisbury Marine Con. Co. Salisbury, Md. 1912	Gas Eng. 4 Cyc. 6 Cyl. 4¾×5½ Herschell-Spillman	R. Albert Barry	Bordentown, N. J. Philadelphia	
2902	Seriola	Wood	Cb TC Aux Sch W&S 12 1050		—	46– 6 32– 6	12– 6	— 2– 8	B. B. Crowninshield Rice Bros. Co. East Boothbay, Me. 1910	Gas Eng. 4 Cyc. 2 Cyl. 6½×8 Sterling 1912	H. B. Day	Wianno Mass.	
2903	Seven Seas	Wood	K TC AuxSch R&L 25 1413	224731	14 20	58– 6 38– 0	12– 0	7– 6 7– 9	Cox & Stevens Bath Iron Works Ltd. Bath, Me. 1925	Gas Eng. 4 Cyc. 4 Cyl. 3¾×5 Scripps	Van S. Merle-Smith	Oyster Bay, L. I. New York	
2904	Sevilla	Wood	K DC Houseboat		—	50– 0 —	20– 0	— 1– 6	Howard Douglas Manhasset Ship Building Co.	....	John E. Hurst	Baltimore, Md.	

Prices for *Sequoia*

1925	Estimated original cost of the yacht	$ 200,000
1928	Sold by Cadwalader to Dunning	?
1931	Sold by Dunning to Department of Commerce	$ 48,860
1935	Sold by Department of Commerce to U.S. Navy	$ 48,860
1977	Sold by U.S. Navy to Malloy	$ 286,000
1978	Sold by Malloy to Pulliam	$ 355,000
1978	Price proposed by a congressman for government to repurchase	$1,000,000
1980	Sold by Pulliam to Ocean Learning Institute (O.L.I.)	$ 750,000
1981	Sold by O.L.I. to Arendsee for Presidential Yacht Trust	$1,100,000
1991	Value estimated for Norshipco by Hull and Cargo Surveyors, Inc.	$3,200,000
1999	Offered for sale by Norshipco	$2,500,000
2000	Sold by Norshipco to Silversmith	$1,900,000
2001	Offered for sale by Silversmith	$3,500,000
2003	Offered for sale by Silversmith	$5,000,000

Author's Notes on John Trumpy's Design for *Sequoia*

Sequoia's fame does not rest solely on her Presidential history, unique as that is, but also because she is a fine example of John Trumpy's designing skills applied to what were known in the 1920s as "house boats." Trumpy used innovations in hull construction that provided unusual strength for a shallow-draft vessel. His design for *Sequoia II* was well conceived for comfortable family living and easy operation in protected waters.

THE HULL

The original Trumpy architectural drawings for *Sequoia* have not been found, at least not by this writing. However, late in 2001 Captain Antonio Gelsi, an Italian master mariner and artist, visited the *Sequoia* at her dock in Washington. He became interested in her design. With the help and encouragement of her skipper, Anthony Wells, he measured her hull construction and produced detailed drawings that showed construction features that until then had not been fully understood by her owner and crew.

Captain Gelsi's drawings show that *Sequoia*'s hull structure is built upon a complex keel package composed of a strong interior keelson topped with an iron rail, or steel stringer. This provides much of the stiffness necessary for her long and narrow hull, which is subject to hogging and sagging forces. It is noteworthy that *Sequoia* does not have watertight bulkheads, nor does she have double planking, features that have been cause for safety concerns by the Secret Service and the Coast Guard.

Spaced along the hull are ten transverse steel bulkheads (called web frames), each joined at right angles to the keelson and supported underneath by 10-inch floor timbers. These bulkheads connect to the longitudinal stringers at the turn of the bilges. Together with the keel, they constitute a strong grid structure that augments *Sequoia*'s ninety-five conventional wood frames.

It can be seen in these drawings that *Sequoia* has a very shallow exterior keel. As may be inferred, this, plus her substantial deck housing, tends to make her tender in beam seas and subject to listing when weights are applied topside. Therefore, she must carry a good measure of interior ballast to give her the stiffness she needs. However, with such a shallow keel, she is also subject to considerable windage, or drift, under beam wind conditions. But there is an obvious advantage in having the shallow exterior keel. If the vessel is grounded when transiting the tidal waters of the Intracoastal Waterway, a shallow keel would not cause serious listing as the tide ebbed.

A particularly graceful and interesting feature of Trumpy's design is what is sometimes referred to as "the ducktail" located just under the overhanging stern below the waterline. It provides a flat horizontal area that helps reduce the "squatting" tendency of such a vessel in shallow waters at and above cruising speed.

THE INTERIOR ACCOMMODATIONS

Without seeing Trumpy's original plans for the interior of *Sequoia,* we can only speculate on how she was originally laid out based on a few photographs and comments from crew members. It is obvious that she has been altered over the years to suit the times and her missions. Original crew member Arne Hauger mentions that the owner's cabin was originally aft, but that has not been documented. In some late 1970s photographs, a companionway appears to be leading from what is now called the "aft salon" down to the aft cabin. That may have been for extra access or egress when *Sequoia* was a static museum, but it has since been removed. We know that an elevator was installed in 1933 at the rear of the main salon for President Roosevelt to descend belowdecks, but we lack information on just how that space under the main deck was arranged for the elevator. Today that space is a head.

THE DECK PLAN

Trumpy designed *Sequoia's* upper deck aft of the stack to accommodate several boats and davits and was not intended for use by guests. The original access was only by a narrow staircase from the service galley. The mast was first located over the middle of the deckhouse instead of behind the stack as it is today. That change was made in the mid-1940s. The deck was cleared and strengthened and equipped with a full railing with easy access by a staircase in the late 1960s. The upper deck was restored and raised about four inches in 1986 to give more headroom on the main deck.

The area just aft of the main salon, often referred to as the "aft salon," was originally designed as an open sitting area under the upper deck, much like a back porch equipped with roll-down curtains. After air-conditioning came into use, that part of the yacht was fully enclosed with removable wooden window panels and doors.

Sequoia's Specifications

Length	Overall, 104 feet 7 inches, length at waterline, 98 feet 11 inches
Beam	19 feet
Draft	4 feet 6 inches
Tonnage	147 gross tons, 133 net tons
Power	Twin 8-71 Detroit diesels, total 870 hp
Propellers	36" diameter, four-bladed, made of bronze
Generators	Two Northern Lights, 50-kilowatt, diesel-powered
Document number	D225115
Builder	Mathis Yacht Building Company, Camden, N.J., 1925
Designer	John Trumpy
Hull construction	Originally 2-inch juniper planking on sawn double oak frames, repaired with fir planks
Deckhouse	Mahogany
Steering	Wheel, cables, pulley, and quadrant
Guest cabins	Three doubles, one single
Water capacity	1,200 gallons
Fuel capacity	Two stainless steel tanks of 750 gallons each
Fuel consumption	Approximately 9 gallons per hour at 8 knots
Speed	Cruising, 8–9 knots; full 10 knots (hull speed, 13.3 knots)
Crew requirements	Captain, engineer, cook/steward, and deckhand

Plan and Profile Drawings of *Sequoia*

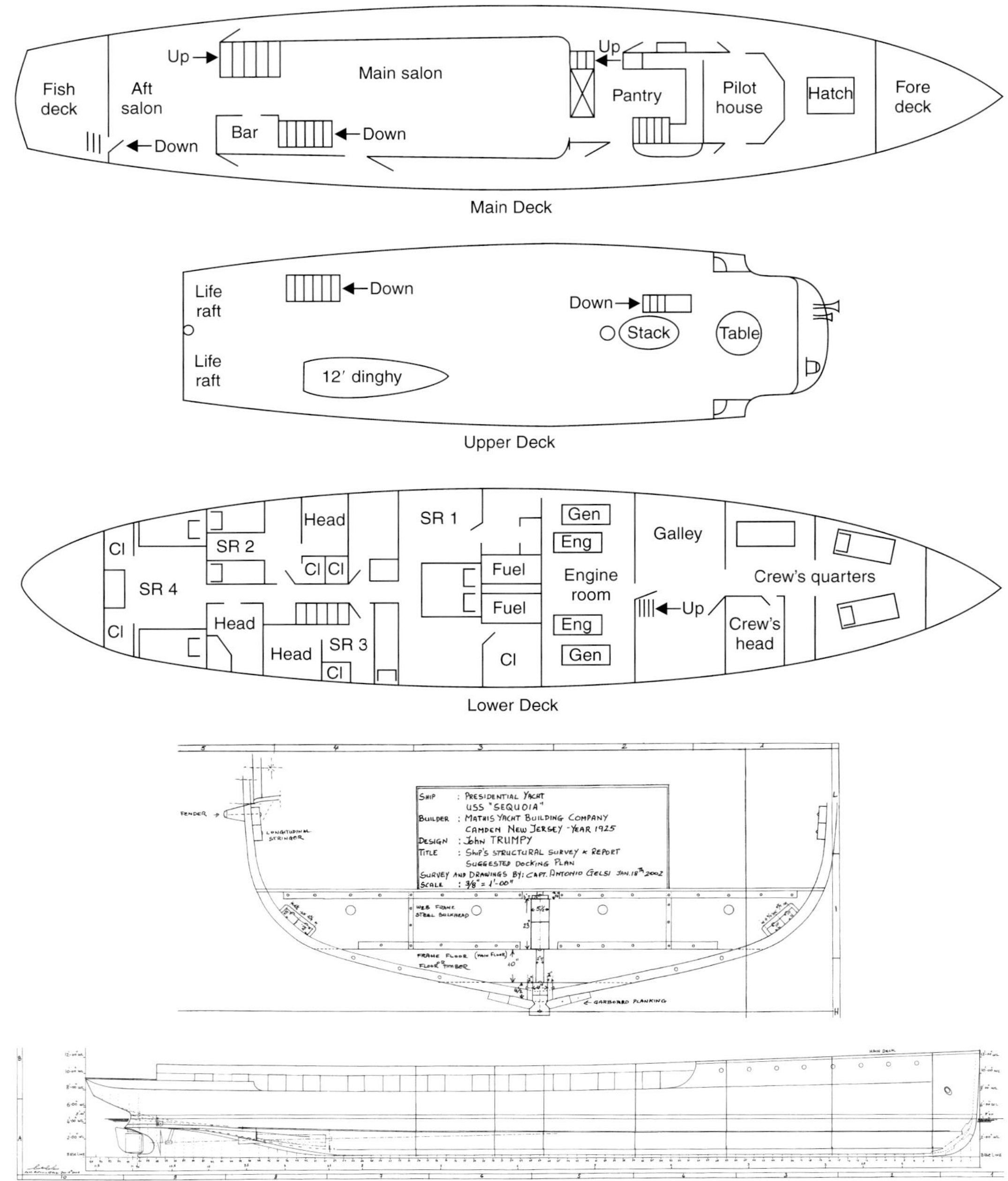

Naval Commanders of *Sequoia,* 1933–77

These service dates of commanding officers and officers-in-charge, 1933–77, are as recorded on a brass plate mounted in the pilothouse of *Sequoia* (presidents and their dates added by the author).

Notes: When the yacht was not in commission but "in service," the commanding officer was designated "officer-in-charge" rather than "commanding officer."

Some officers-in-charge of *Sequoia* were also in charge of the Navy Administrative Unit at the Navy Yard, which included *Sequoia,* other naval craft, and the navy stewards assigned to the White House and Camp David.

Jerauld Wright became a full admiral.

J.H. Besson, Jr., became a rear admiral.

Roosevelt 1933–45	Lt. (j.g.) J.S. Blue	March 1933–November 1933
	Lt. Cmdr. Jerauld Wright	December 1935–June 1936
	Lt. R.L. Campbell, Jr.	June 1936–April 1937
	Lt. N.W. Sears	April 1937–October 1939
	Lt. R.H. Rice	October 1939–June 1941
	Lt. Cmdr. W.V. Pratt II	June 1941–January 1943
	Lt. Cmdr. J. H. Besson, Jr.	March 1943–October 1943
Truman 1945–53	Cmdr. J.W. Payne, Jr.	April 1944–January 1945
	Cmdr. T.H. Connor	May 1946–December 1948
	Lt. Cmdr. E.H. Winslow	December 1948–January 1951
	Lt. R.K. Rosemont	January 1951–December 1952
Eisenhower 1953–61	Lt. R.A. Bowling	December 1952–September 1954
	Lt. W.H. Meanix	September 1954–April 1957
	Lt. Cmdr. J.P. Duckett	April 1957–October 1959
Kennedy 1961–63	Lt. Cmdr. D. Meek	October 1959–July 1962
	Lt. Cmdr. A.P. Ismay	July 1962–July 1964
Johnson 1963–69	Lt. Cmdr. C.J. Beasley	July 1964–July 1966
	Lt. Cmdr. T.F. Morgan	July 1966–June 1968
	Lt. Cmdr. L.M. Moore	June 1968–August 1969
Nixon 1969–74	Lt. Cmdr. R.A. Johnson	August 1969–September 1971
	Lt. Cmdr. G.B. Phillips	September 1971–January 1973
	Lt. Cmdr. A.J. Combe	January 1973–August 1974
Ford 1974–77	Lt. Cmdr. J.L. O'Brien	August 1974–April 1976
	Lt. Cmdr. D.E. Beliech, Jr.	April 1976–June 1977

A Sample Page from the 1935 Logbook of USS *Sequoia*

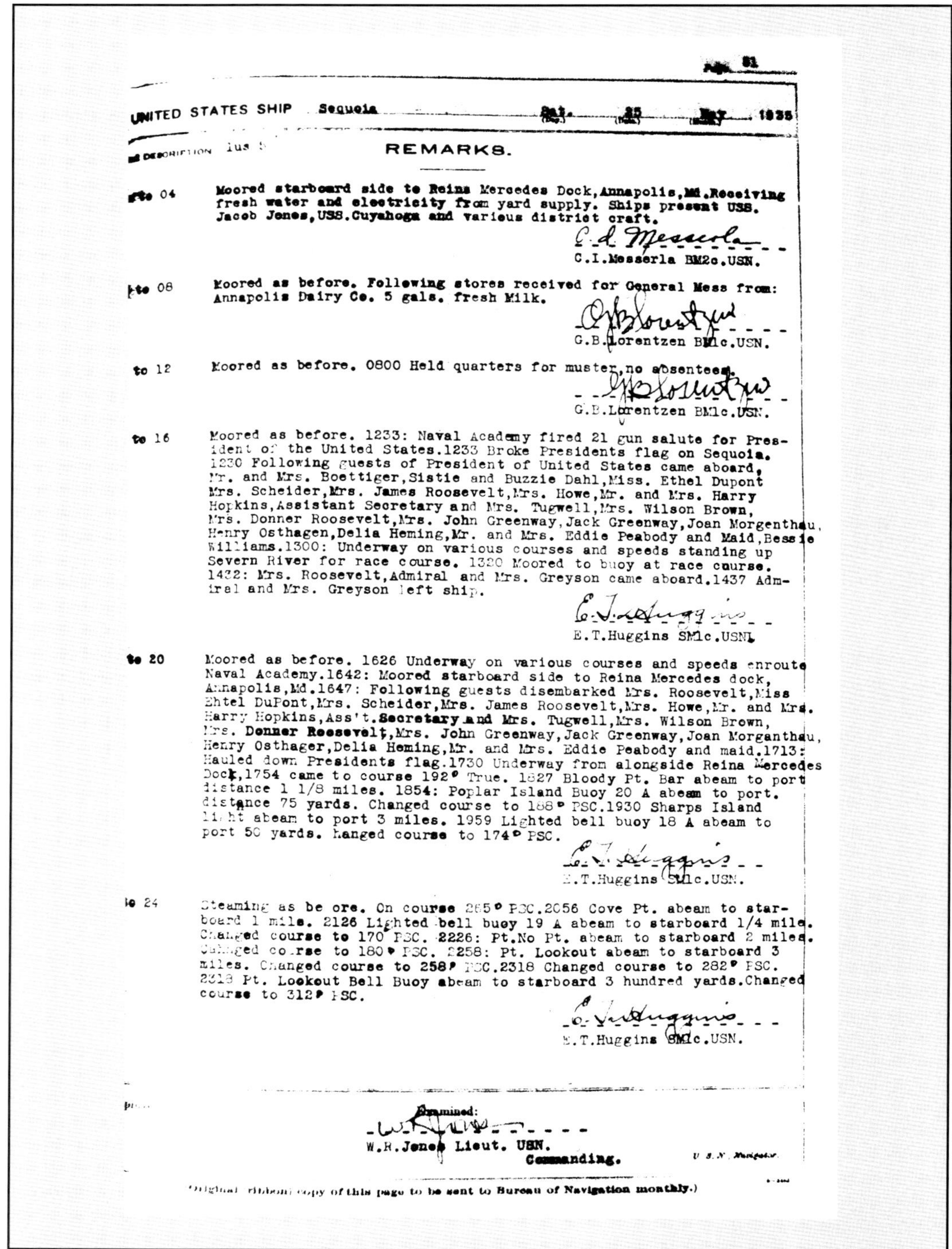

Page 81

UNITED STATES SHIP Sequoia Sat. 25 May 1935

REMARKS.

to 04 Moored starboard side to Reina Mercedes Dock, Annapolis, Md. Receiving fresh water and electricity from yard supply. Ships present USS. Jacob Jones, USS. Cuyahoga and various district craft.

C.I.Messerla BM2c.USN.

to 08 Moored as before. Following stores received for General Mess from: Annapolis Dairy Co. 5 gals. fresh Milk.

G.B.Lorentzen BM1c.USN.

to 12 Moored as before. 0800 Held quarters for muster, no absentees.

G.B.Lorentzen BM1c.USN.

to 16 Moored as before. 1233: Naval Academy fired 21 gun salute for President of the United States. 1233 Broke Presidents flag on Sequoia. 1230 Following guests of President of United States came aboard, Mr. and Mrs. Boettiger, Sistie and Buzzie Dahl, Miss. Ethel Dupont Mrs. Scheider, Mrs. James Roosevelt, Mrs. Howe, Mr. and Mrs. Harry Hopkins, Assistant Secretary and Mrs. Tugwell, Mrs. Wilson Brown, Mrs. Donner Roosevelt, Mrs. John Greenway, Jack Greenway, Joan Morgenthau, Henry Osthagen, Delia Heming, Mr. and Mrs. Eddie Peabody and Maid, Bessie Williams. 1300: Underway on various courses and speeds standing up Severn River for race course. 1320 Moored to buoy at race course. 1432: Mrs. Roosevelt, Admiral and Mrs. Greyson came aboard. 1437 Admiral and Mrs. Greyson left ship.

E.T.Huggins SM1c.USN.

to 20 Moored as before. 1626 Underway on various courses and speeds enroute Naval Academy. 1642: Moored starboard side to Reina Mercedes dock, Annapolis, Md. 1647: Following guests disembarked Mrs. Roosevelt, Miss Ehtel DuPont, Mrs. Scheider, Mrs. James Roosevelt, Mrs. Howe, Mr. and Mrs. Harry Hopkins, Ass't. Secretary and Mrs. Tugwell, Mrs. Wilson Brown, Mrs. Donner Roosevelt, Mrs. John Greenway, Jack Greenway, Joan Morganthau, Henry Osthager, Delia Heming, Mr. and Mrs. Eddie Peabody and maid. 1713: Hauled down Presidents flag. 1730 Underway from alongside Reina Mercedes Dock, 1754 came to course 192° True. 1827 Bloody Pt. Bar abeam to port distance 1 1/8 miles. 1854: Poplar Island Buoy 20 A abeam to port. distance 75 yards. Changed course to 188° PSC. 1930 Sharps Island light abeam to port 3 miles. 1959 Lighted bell buoy 18 A abeam to port 50 yards. Changed course to 174° PSC.

E.T.Huggins SM1c.USN.

to 24 Steaming as before. On course 265° PSC. 2056 Cove Pt. abeam to starboard 1 mile. 2126 Lighted bell buoy 19 A abeam to starboard 1/4 mile. Changed course to 170 PSC. 2226: Pt. No Pt. abeam to starboard 2 miles. Changed course to 180° PSC. 2258: Pt. Lookout abeam to starboard 3 miles. Changed course to 258° PSC. 2318 Changed course to 282° PSC. 2318 Pt. Lookout Bell Buoy abeam to starboard 3 hundred yards. Changed course to 312° PSC.

E.T.Huggins SM1c.USN.

Examined:

W.R.Jones Lieut. USN.
Commanding.

U. S. N., Navigator.

(Original (ribbon) copy of this page to be sent to Bureau of Navigation monthly.)

Rendering Honors Passing George Washington's Tomb

U.S. Navy Regulations, Article 2185:

When a ship of the navy is passing Washington's tomb . . . the following ceremonies shall be observed in so far as may be practicable: The full guard and band shall be paraded, the bell tolled, and the national ensign half-masted at the beginning of the tolling of the bell. When opposite Washington's tomb, the guard shall present arms, persons on deck shall salute, facing in the direction of the tomb, and "Taps" shall be sounded. The national ensign shall be two-blocked and the tolling shall cease at the last note of "Taps," after which the national anthem shall be played. Upon completion of the national anthem, "Carry on" shall be sounded.

Note: The custom aboard *Sequoia,* which had no band or guard, was simply to toll the bell, half-mast the ensign, and sound "Taps," at which time all hands saluted and civilians placed their right hand over their heart. When "Taps" and the tolling ceased, the ensign was two-blocked (hoisted up again) and a recording of the "Star-Spangled Banner" was played, followed by the order "Carry on."

Government Designations of *Sequoia,* 1931–77

1931: March 24, "Inspection Vessel," Department of Commerce, Bureau of Marine Inspection and Navigation.

1933: March 25, commissioned as "USS *Sequoia,* (AG 23)" (stands for auxiliary general) as "the Presidential Yacht."

1933: November 16, "in service" (for yard overhaul).

1935: April 1, "in commission" (for presidential use).

1935: July 27, for three days, temporarily "in service" status.

1935: August 1, "in commission" (for presidential use).

1935: December 9, "in service" (during three winter months).

1936: March 2, assigned as the secretary of the navy's yacht (AG 23) and available to senior government officals. She was used as such by Presidents Truman, Kennedy, and Johnson.

1969: January 1, assigned as presidential yacht.

1969: June 1, assigned as the secretary of the navy's yacht, but under the direct control of the White House. She was used by Presidents Nixon and Ford and was available to other senior government officials until sold in 1977.

Note: Only naval ships in commission carry the designation "USS." However, after *Sequoia* was decommissioned and "in service," both inside and outside the navy she was often, if erroneously, referred to as "USS *Sequoia,*" much the way a retired governor continues to be addressed as "governor" after he leaves office. She also was known as "the yacht *Sequoia,*" "the naval yacht," "the presidential yacht," and "the secretary of the navy's yacht."

Source: Naval Historical Center

Concurrent Resolution

99TH CONGRESS
1ST SESSION

S. CON. RES. 98

To recognize the historical significance of the former Presidential yacht Sequoia, and express support for her donation to the United States Navy by the Presidential Yacht Trust.

IN THE SENATE OF THE UNITED STATES

DECEMBER 18 (legislative day, DECEMBER 16), 1985

Mr. GARN (for Mr. SIMPSON) (for himself and Mr. CRANSTON) submitted the following concurrent resolution; which was considered and agreed to

---

CONCURRENT RESOLUTION

To recognize the historical significance of the former Presidential yacht Sequoia, and express support for her donation to the United States Navy by the Presidential Yacht Trust.

Whereas the former Presidential yacht Sequoia served eight Presidents of the United States, from Herbert Hoover to Gerald R. Ford, over a period of forty-five years;

Whereas the Sequoia was the setting for Presidential meetings, negotiations and decisions of extraordinary significance for and effect on the history of the United States and the course of world events;

Whereas the Sequoia was disposed of in 1977 to reduce Federal expenditures;

Whereas in recognition of Sequoia's unique historical significance, the private, bipartisan, and nonprofit Presidential

2

Yacht Trust was established in 1981 for the purpose of restoring and preserving Sequoia;

Whereas since 1981 many Americans have visited the Sequoia and demonstrated support for her preservation and return to service;

Whereas in response to this support, the Presidential Yacht Trust, in consultation with the United States Navy, has determined that the proper future of the Sequoia is her return to Government service in the United States Navy as the Presidential yacht; and

Whereas the Presidential Yacht Trust has taken steps to fully restore the Sequoia by November 15, 1988, to donate her to the Navy as a gift of the Presidential Yacht Trust and the American people, and to establish an endowment sufficient for her future operation and maintenance: Now, therefore, be it

Resolved by the Senate (the House of Representatives concurring), That Congress—

(1) recognizes the unique significance of the former Presidential yacht Sequoia which has made her a symbol of American political heritage and the Office of the President;

(2) supports the plans of the Presidential Yacht Trust to donate the Sequoia, with an endowment sufficient for her operations and maintenance, to the United States Navy for service once again as the Presidential yacht.

O

SCON 98 ATS

Letter from William L. Ball, III, Assistant to the President, Concerning Preservation of *Sequoia*

THE WHITE HOUSE

WASHINGTON

June 20, 1986

Dear Senator Simpson:

I am pleased to forward to you the attached White House Statement concerning the former Presidential yacht SEQUOIA.

In brief, the statement indicates that the President joins with the Congress in both recognizing the unique historical significance of the SEQUOIA and in supporting the plans for her preservation and return to official service without expense to the American taxpayers.

Sincerely,

William L. Ball, III

The Honorable Alan K. Simpson
United States Senate
Washington, D.C. 20510

Endnotes

Chapter 2. *Sequoia's* Presidential Predecessors, 1880–1929

1. For more details on early yachts see *Presidential Yachts* by Roy C. Smith III published in *Shipmate* May 1985; also *Special Fleet, The History of the Presidential Yachts* by Fred E. Crockett, Down East Books, Camden, Maine, 1985.

Chapter 3. First Call to Presidential Service, 1931–35

1. A photo of this so-called presidential vessel is held in CORBIS photo archives. It could accommodate only eight passengers and carried a crew of five.

Chapter 4. Secretary of the Navy's Yacht, 1936–68

1. *Forrestal Diaries,* 200 and 292.
2. Herbert L. Pankratz, archivist at the Eisenhower Library, provided this information in a letter to the author dated September 1989.
3. Based on a letter by Captain R.A. Bowling, USN (Ret.), dated March 17, 2003, and on a letter to the author from Herbert L. Pankratz, archivist at the Eisenhower Library, dated May 22, 2003.
4. Based on a memoir provided to former crew members by Willie (Boone) Boyd, who was a Boatswain Mate third class aboard *Sequoia,* 1954–56.
5. A more detailed version of the party can be found in *Grace and Power* by Sally Bedell Smith, p. 363.
6. *Naval Institute Oral History,* Kerr series, 445.

Chapter 5. Again the President's Yacht, 1968–77

1. Bureau of Ships memo dated August 17, 1965, regarding the requested alterations.
2. Letter to officer-in-charge, *Sequoia,* on stability from chief, Bureau of Ships, 1966.
3. From a three-page pamphlet describing *Sequoia* issued by the Naval Station, Washington, D.C., 1966.
4. Interview reported in *Imperial Beach Star News,* California, January 8, 1987.
5. *Washington Post,* September 10, 1966, section B1.
6. Kissinger, *The White House Years,* 1174–5.
7. Walter Isaacson, *Kissinger, A Biography,* 417.
8. Kissinger, 498.
9. Ibid., 553, 577.
10. In August 1972, Nixon received a gift from Brezhnev in the form of a fast Russian hydrofoil that was delivered aboard a Russian freighter to Baltimore. It was described in the *Washington Evening Star* as specially equipped for presidential use, having

wolf-fur carpeting, a swivel chair, a table inlaid with a painting of the USS *Constitution,* and a bar equipped with brandy cups of Georgian silver. This was in return for the Cadillac limousine Nixon had given to Brezhnev on his visit to Moscow earlier that same year. There seems to be no record of Nixon ever using this presidential hydrofoil, but Soviet Ambassador Dobrynin and Henry Kissinger were seen enjoying a ride in it on the Potomac River.

11. Pierre Elliott Trudeau, *Memoirs,* 219.
12. President Ford in a letter to Timothy L. Besmer, Sr. (by permission).

Chapter 6. *Sequoia* in the Private Sector, 1977–81

1. Carter was quoted in *Antiquities & Arts Weekly,* March 21, 1980, as having made this statement.
2. An explanation contained in a letter issued by the Defense Logistics Agency on May 12, 1977.
3. Reported by United Press International on May 5, 1977.
4. Ibid.
5. Reported in the *New York Times,* May 12, 1978.
6. As told to the author in an interview with Captain Chapman in 1983.

Chapter 7. Presidential Yacht Trust, 1981–88

1. Letter to the trust from Senator Strom Thurmond, dated August 4, 1981.
2. Contained in a letter to the author from Dean Rusk, dated July 20, 1987.
3. More details on this cruise can be found in "Yacht of Presidents," *Yachting Magazine,* September 1985, by the author.
4. See "S.CON. Res. 98" of the 99th Congress (1985) in appendix for complete text.
5. Assistant to the President, William L. Ball wrote to Senator Alan Simpson on June 20, 1986, stating in part that the president joins in supporting plans for returning *Sequoia* to official service.
6. As reported in a Naval District, Washington, D.C., Memorandum for the Record, dated July 1988.
7. Memorandum for the president from the secretary of defense, undated.
8. From a report in the *Wall Street Journal,* October 6, 1988, and from a report in the *Washington Post,* August 29, 1989.

Chapter 8. Seeking a Course for *Sequoia,* 1998–2004

1. Based on the author's conversation with R. Josh Lanier in 2003.
2. *Sequoia* was advertised with her photo in *Architectural Digest* during 2002 in a section called "Extraordinary Properties on the Market."
3. This editorial appeared in the *New York Times,* September 16, 2003, written by Stephen S. Pickering of the *New York Times* staff.

Bibliography

Ambrose, Stephen E. *Nixon, The Triumph of a Politician, 1962–1972.* New York: Simon & Schuster, 1989.

Browning, G. "Salvaging the Ship of State." *Washington Post,* August 21, 1989.

Crockett, Fred E. *Special Fleet: The History of the Presidential Yachts.* Camden, Maine: Down East Books, 1985.

Eisenhower, Julie Nixon. *Special People.* New York: Simon & Schuster, 1977.

Farnsworth, Clyde H. "The Ebb and Flow of *Sequoia's* Fortunes." The *New York Times,* November 23, 1986.

Fay, Paul B., Jr. *The Pleasure of His Company.* New York: Harper & Row, 1966.

Haller, Henry. *The White House Family Cookbook.* New York: Random House, 1987.

Head, I. L. and P.E. Trudeau. *The Canadian Way.* Toronto, Ontario, Canada: McClelland & Stewart, Inc., 1995.

Isaacson, Walter. *Kissinger: A Biography.* New York: Simon and Schuster, 1992.

Kelly, Giles M. "Yacht of Presidents." *Yachting.* September 1985.

Kissinger, Henry. *The White House Years.* Boston: Little Brown, 1979.

Lawford, Valentine. "The Presidential Yacht USS *Sequoia,* Restoring a Time Honored American Tradition." *Architectural Digest,* January 1993.

Millis, Walter, ed. *The Forrestal Diaries.* New York: Viking Press, 1951.

Money, James L., ed. *Dictionary of American Naval Fighting Ships.* vols. II and VI, Washington, D.C.: Naval Historical Center, 1968.

Niven, David. *The Moon's a Balloon.* New York: Putnam, 1972.

Pickering, Stephen S. "Presidential Yacht *Sequoia,* A Piece of Historic Furniture Deserves a Permanent Safe Harbor." The *New York Times,* September 16, 2002.

Pollack, J. M. "*Sequoia,* A Most Political Yacht." *Nautical Quarterly,* Fall 1982.

Rogon, Lee. "The President's Yacht." *The New Yorker,* January 3, 1953.

Ship's History File, Ships' History Division. Naval Historical Center. Washington Navy Yard, Washington, D.C.

Smith, Sally Bedell. *Grace and Power.* New York: Random House, 2004.

Szostek, M. "*Sequoia:* Fitting out the Presidential Yacht." *All Hands,* September 1975.

Taylor, Blaine, "*Sequoia:* The Yacht that Served Eight Presidents." *Sea Classics,* March 1996.

Taylor, Roger C. "The Mathis-Trumpy Story." *Wooden Boat,* November-December, 1996.

Tolf, R. *Trumpy.* St. Michaels, Md.: Tiller Publishing, 1996.

Trudeau, P. E. *Memoirs.* Toronto, Ontario, Canada: McClelland & Stewart, Inc., 1993.

Index